Successful enquiry answering every time

Successful enquiry answering every time

Thinking your way from problem to solution

The seventh edition of Tim Buckley Owen's classic *Success at the Enquiry Desk*

Fully revised and updated

Tim Buckley Owen

facet
publishing

© Tim Buckley Owen 1996, 1997, 1998, 2000, 2003, 2006, 2012, 2017

Published by Facet Publishing
7 Ridgmount Street, London WC1E 7AE
www.facetpublishing.co.uk

Facet Publishing is wholly owned by CILIP: the Library and Information Association.

British Library Cataloguing in Publication Data
A catalogue record for this book is available from the British Library.

ISBN 978-1-78330-193-5 (paperback)
ISBN 978-1-78330-194-2 (hardback)
ISBN 978-1-78330-215-4 (e-book)

First published 1996.
This seventh edition, 2017.

Text printed on FSC accredited material.

Typeset from author's files in 11/14 pt Minion and Myriad by Flagholme Publishing Services.
Printed and made in Great Britain by CPI Group (UK) Ltd, Croydon, CR0 4YY.

Dedication

To Rufus. The future starts here.

Contents

Introduction

Why thinking skills matter

Twenty-one years ago – almost to the day actually – I rented a small holiday cottage on the Isle of Wight, hired a large and clunky computer from a local firm (for rather more than the cost of renting the cottage) and settled down to draft the first edition of this book. At that time I never thought there would be a second edition, let alone a seventh.

Since then, some things have come full circle. We now live on the Island most of the time, so it's here again that this edition has been penned. But when it comes to the information profession – the people whose job is to answer enquiries for a living – it's difficult to decide whether we're talking about a straight road from the book-lined room to a world of virtual crowdsourced content or, again, about a situation where things have come full circle.

Let me explain. When people want to satisfy their immediate curiosity these days they're much more likely to turn to social media on their mobile device than ask their local library. So the days of flesh and blood intervention in this kind of quick reference enquiry are inevitably numbered.

But the professional skills that underpin them are not. They keep coming round and they work for anyone whose job is to provide information, advice and guidance using third party sources to help them. So they're also transferrable skills, relevant not only in libraries but also for anyone whose job is to provide learning support to students, work with research teams or offer contact centre services.

In my work as a trainer, I'm increasingly being asked to develop modules and courses that address new value-added activities, and particularly in taking the process beyond the traditional outcome: delivery of raw literature search results with no further comment. Clients for this kind of training include specialist organizations of all kinds, government, law firms and, most recently, health bodies.

So although the book's coverage of the underlying skills remains fundamentally the same, I felt that at least some of the emphasis needed to change. Particularly in the later chapters, there's now much more focus on the information professional's role in things like fostering information literacy, managing the desk research process and presenting research results effectively. These things matter, I believe, whether you're actually doing them – as a legal or health information specialist, for example – or supporting others – working with students doing their assignments or members of the public trying to make sense of what they find on the web.

First published when the internet was little more than a demonstration project, and the fax and microfiche were far more widely used than e-mail or the cloud, the book has developed over the years to take account of every technological development that has impacted on the enquiry process – including social media, mobile communications and the exponential expansion of images as potential sources of information.

But its strength lies in the fact that it has never been technology-led. Instead it has used technology as the enabler of the thought processes that information professionals need to engage in when handling enquiries, and it has worked on the principle that new technology doesn't render the information professional irrelevant but raises the skill stakes. We now use the same tools as our users – so our job is to use those tools much more efficiently.

How? Well, mainly by exercising our thinking skills. At every stage in the journey from initial unformed enquiry to polished, value-added answer, we can deploy a different thinking discipline to help us on our way.

In Chapter 1, we can use our analytical thinking skills to try to bring some order to the enquirer's perhaps rather incoherent or incomplete request. And when we're deprived of the opportunity to see or even hear the enquirer because they're elsewhere (as in Chapter 2) we can try to keep them on-side by thinking empathetically.

Imagination is the thinking skill we bring to bear in Chapter 3, when the enquirer is waiting for us to come up with a solution and we're trying to fight down the panic because we haven't a clue where to start. Then in Chapter 4, when we have finally decided what to do and are developing – or advising on – a possible search strategy, that's when we need to be able to think systematically.

Inevitably things go wrong from time to time and the answer is just nowhere to be found – so that's when we need to come at the problem sideways, using lateral thinking to produce an ingenious alternative, as covered in Chapter 5.

By contrast, Chapter 6 is about success, where creative thinking can help us, or the library users we're advising, to present the answer really well.

With both academic librarians and researchers particularly in mind, a brand new Chapter 7 takes this process a stage further, looking at how your critical thinking skills can help turn raw search results into an authoritative narrative answer that a researcher can hand over to their client or a student to their tutor. And in Chapter 8, we think about reaching decisions on things like which enquiry tracking or reference management software or discovery tools to go for and – crucially – the multipurpose reference sources we'll need to get us started on a variety of enquiries. We also look here at how best to deploy our three fundamental resources: our time, our intellect and our employer's money. All this requires predictive thinking, where we try to anticipate our enquirers' needs.

Of course, none of this could happen without a great deal of input and support from some pretty knowledgeable people. I'm especially grateful to Phil Bradley for his expertise on search engines and searching in general, and to Caroline De Brún for her invaluable advice on reference management software. The book would also have been the poorer if I'd not been able to draw on Karen Blakeman's knowledge of internet searching, and Paul Pedley's experience in copyright and legal issues. Other reviewers have kindly agreed to Facet's request to look at some of the chapters in draft, and for their comments I am also very grateful. You know who you are.

At Facet Publishing itself, Damian Mitchell has been patience and courtesy personified as I've pestered him over details and schedules, as has the book's project manager Lin Franklin. And I must say a special thank-you, too, to Facet's Helen Carley. It was she who persuaded me – in the face of considerable reluctance on my part, I might add – to write the book in the first place over two decades ago, and her unwavering confidence in it ever since has buoyed me up through its many editions.

As for my wife Barbara, who has read every word of the more recent editions in draft and offered her invaluable comments, I've said it before and I'll say it again: I know I frequently resist your advice, darling, but I almost always end up taking it. And finally, a great big thank-you to all the hundreds of people who've attended my training courses over the years. If you're one of them and are reading the book now, you might possibly recognize one of your own ideas in there – because I steal course participants' ideas shamelessly all the time. Without them, I don't think any of this could have happened and, again, I'm very grateful.

So I hope you find some useful things in the book that you can apply, that it makes you think about what you do and how you do it – and that it sometimes makes you laugh. Enjoy!

Tim Buckley Owen

Eight essential thinking skills for successful enquiry answering

1 **Analytical**: Never take an enquiry at face value, always ask a question back – because you never know where it may lead.
2 **Empathetic**: With remote enquiries you are deprived of most of the clues that we take for granted when dealing with people face to face – so make sure you really do understand what they want.
3 **Imaginative**: Start by imagining what the final answer will look like – that will help you focus on the best sources and delivery media for the job.
4 **Systematic**: Your enquirer has access to the same search engines as you – your job is to add value by using professionally edited sources and smarter searching.
5 **Lateral**: If you can't find the answer, ask yourself who really needs to know this – that should give you ideas for who to ask for help.
6 **Creative**: Make sure you always add value when presenting your answer – that will demonstrate your professionalism.
7 **Critical**: Looking beyond the raw search results is an ever-more important part of your job.
8 **Predictive**: Decide on the tools you need to acquire by anticipating your users' needs.

CHAPTER 1

What do they really want?

Using your analytical thinking skills to understand the question

In this chapter you'll find out how to:

- **avoid misunderstandings**
- **ask the right questions**
- **agree the task**
- **find out how long you've got to do it**
- **deploy your analytical thinking skills.**

Picture the scene. You're in the kitchen getting ready for a dinner party and you think your partner has just said: 'Have you got the time?' So you could reply: 'It's ten to eight and the guests are going to be here any moment, so let's get on with it.' Or you could say: 'Do you mean what time is it now or how long does it take to cook?' To which your partner replies patiently: 'No, darling – did you remember to buy the thyme?'

By simply telling your partner the time you'll have taken the question at face value. But by answering the question with a question you'll have dealt with any potential misunderstanding from the outset – and in this case, misunderstanding there certainly was. The question used in this little domestic drama was a forced choice question – one of several specific question types, each of which can be deployed for a particular purpose. In this instance, it helped to defuse a little bit of potential personal strife. When you use this and other questioning techniques at work, it can save you a deal of trouble from the outset.

You'll deal with many of your enquirers orally, face to face. The possibilities for misunderstandings are endless – accent, articulation, assumptions, all can send you scurrying off in totally the wrong direction, wasting both your time and the enquirer's. But with face-to-face enquiries, you are at least offered lots of clues; most of what we communicate is non-verbal, so you are able to glean what you can from facial expression, eye contact, body language. But you are deprived of these clues when your queries come in by phone, and you have even less to go on when they arrive in written form – by e-mail or text for instance. We'll look at remote enquiry handling in Chapter 2 – but right now, let's assume that the enquirer is standing in front of you. In our journey from what the enquirer asked to what they actually wanted to know, we need to deploy our analytical thinking skills.

Avoiding misunderstandings

So the first task has to be: always make sure you understand the question. And in almost all cases this means answering a question with a question – a supplementary. There'll be plenty of times when you think the meaning behind the question is obvious. Beware! This happens far less often than you imagine. It has to be as simple a question as 'Where's the toilet?' for you to forgo a supplementary safely. In most other instances, you have to assume that there's more you can learn about the enquirer's needs by questioning a bit further. If you get it wrong, it'll be your fault no matter how unhelpful the enquirer has been. You are the professional, remember, and the enquirer is the amateur.

Take a look at the set of typical enquiries shown on the next page. You may as well get used to them because we'll be following their progress from initial mystery to triumphant value-added solution throughout most of the rest of this book. None of them are quite what they seem – and in each case we've given you a clue as to what the problem might be.

Most of these are based on real enquiries, some are exaggerations. (The last one is almost – but not quite – fictional.) However, they all pose real dangers. Rule number one of enquiry answering is that people almost never ask the question to which they really want to know the answer. There are all sorts of reasons for this.

Disgruntled and unconvinced enquirers

They may not want to bother the staff. It's true, a big public or college library can be a busy place. You can have a queue building up just when Maisie decides to go off for coffee. When you're under pressure, it's always a

Enquiry	Clue
Do you have any books on retailing?	This seems very broad and general. Does the enquirer actually need something a bit more specific?
Where do you keep the latest *New Scientist*?	The enquirer seems to know exactly what they want. Do they really though?
I'm looking for information on migration patterns in whales.	Have you heard this correctly?
Do you have the *Electrical Register*?	You may have heard the enquirer correctly this time. But is it really what they meant to say?
I'm trying to find a song called *When I Would Sing Under the Ocean*.	Seems a straightforward enough enquiry with plenty of places to look for the answer. But what if you can't find it anywhere?
Have you got any books on Kew Gardens? That's to say, something on the Crystal Palace, if you can manage it. What would be really helpful, actually, would be the index to the *Illustrated London News*. Or, better still, a book on tropical fish.	Wow! That's quite an extraordinary list of requirements. Are they linked – and, if so, how?
Is it still possible to find information not using the internet?	Well the short answer to this question is 'Yes'. But why is the enquirer asking?

temptation to take an enquiry at face value and answer the question actually put to you. Resist it! You're almost certain to have a disgruntled customer when they realize that you've sent them somewhere that doesn't actually meet their needs.

They may return to the enquiry desk before too long, complaining that you haven't really helped them. They may try to ask someone else instead – a passing member of library staff or a fellow student or colleague who happens to be in there for instance. Or they may simply walk out. Whatever happens as a result, it's a waste of everybody's time, and really bad customer relations.

At the very least, you want them to come back and see you if they're not satisfied, so you can do something to limit the damage. But this isn't necessarily all that easy. You may well be busy with another enquirer when they return, so not only will they be growing more and more impatient, but you'll quite possibly be able to see them out of the corner of your eye, which means you might stop paying full attention to the enquirer you're dealing with now – and risk ending up with two disgruntled customers. You may have gone off shift in the meantime, leaving a colleague to placate the enquirer, who now has to start all over again with their query. And what if you work in a library where they've abolished the enquiry desk altogether and just have roaming staff? Of course your managers will need to have a procedure for retrieving enquirers who are dissatisfied or want more help – but the best solution is to avoid this happening by asking all the right questions in the first place.

Sceptical enquirers

Equally alarming is the kind of enquirer who lacks confidence in your ability to answer the question. They'd sooner browse themselves, perhaps inefficiently, than risk having their time wasted by you. This kind of enquirer should be sending alarm signals both to you and to your boss. It probably means that they've had bad experiences before – either with your service or somewhere else. Either way, it's up to you to convince them, quickly, that you can help, even if you don't know anything about the subject they are interested in. This doesn't mean trying to pull the wool over their eyes – that's the worst possible tactic. You're bound to get found out, and you'll just reinforce the enquirer's scepticism. There are ways of being helpful, even if you haven't a clue what the enquirer is talking about.

Secretive enquirers

Then there are enquirers who just don't want anyone to know what they're doing. These can be the most infuriating kind. Despite your gentle persuasion, they resolutely refuse to disclose any information that might help you to help them. But you must suppress your urge to get annoyed. That will only make matters worse. They may have excellent reasons for not wanting to give anything away. It might be a colleague applying for a job who doesn't want your current employer to get wind of it. It might be an academic who doesn't want to be beaten to publication by a rival. Or would *you* want everyone to know that you were looking for information on sexually transmitted infections?

Time-wasters

You'll also come across people who want to burden you with every tiny detail of their investigation, together with the complete life stories of all their sisters, cousins and aunts. Hobbyist genealogical enquirers frequently fall into this category. You owe it to your other enquirers to steer this type to the point as quickly as possible. They'll try to persuade you that you can't possibly help them without a full understanding of their needs. They may genuinely believe this, or they may simply have time on their hands, and be looking for someone to talk to. Either way, you have to focus them, tactfully.

Equally pernicious are students who try to get you to do their assignments for them. They may come back time and time again trying to get you to look up things that they should really be researching for themselves. This is actually a type of potentially time-wasting activity that you can turn into a benefit. You can seize such opportunities to show them how they can search more efficiently and evaluate the sources they find. (We'll look at aspects of this in later chapters: smarter searching in Chapter 4; evaluating sources in Chapter 6; and making sense of raw search results in Chapter 7.) Sure, coaching them in efficient searching and information management techniques takes time – but if it helps improve their information literacy, it's time invested, not time wasted.

Complaining or angry enquirers

And there will inevitably be times when – despite your best efforts perhaps – you find yourself dealing with enquirers who aren't going to be satisfied whatever you do. They may have a genuine grievance or they may simply be impatient, unreasonable or confrontational by nature. We're going to look at these sorts of challenge in more detail in Chapter 2, where you're dealing with enquirers who you can't see, or perhaps even hear either, because they're communicating with you remotely. It's frankly a lot easier for people to be rude or aggressive by slamming down the phone or flaming someone in an e-mail than it is to have a row face to face. But face-to-face rows you will inevitably encounter from time to time.

So in this chapter, watch out for techniques you can use to reassure the enquirer and gain their confidence. There are masses of them, and they're likely to be more effective than any amount of sweet-talking would be. Many of them draw on your interpersonal skills. You'll need to be approachable, reassuring, discreet, tactful, and frequently firm as well. But underlying your natural human qualities you also need some pretty hard-nosed strategy – a game plan. And this all applies not just when you're dealing with enquirers who present difficulties, but also those from different cultures, or those who are dealing with the challenges of disability. So . . .

Enquirers from different cultural backgrounds

In a multiracial, multicultural society, dealing with people from different cultural backgrounds is simply part of normal life. So making such people feel at their ease in the library or information centre should be second nature. If, for example, you're helping someone who isn't using their first language, you could respond helpfully by using shorter sentences, and perhaps also by using active rather than passive constructions. If you're having difficulty understanding their accent and having to ask them to repeat things, be aware of how your own unspoken communication is coming back to them. Are you maintaining appropriate eye contact, smiling when it feels right and using body language that is encouraging, not threatening or defensive?

Observe and learn from your enquirer, too. When they speak, are they laying the emphasis on different words from the ones you might choose? Are their non-verbal responses to you – eye contact, smiling, facial expression, gestures, even how close they stand – different from what you would expect from someone of your own culture? If so, learn from that too and accommodate it quickly. This is of course a matter of simple courtesy and good manners – but putting your enquirer at their ease in this way also ensures that you can get onto the business of helping them effectively as quickly as possible.

Enquirers with disabilities

People with disabilities expect equivalent consideration. If you're helping someone who's deaf, face them directly and articulate clearly when you speak (without falling into the patronizing and insulting trap of shouting, of course). Bear in mind, too, that they may actually tend to think more visually than orally, and be ready to accommodate that in the way you present information to them. With someone with a visual impairment, try to find out quickly about any special reading requirements they may have and any assistive technology they may be using, and build this into your decisions about how to help them with their enquiry.

Enquirers with speech impediments may feel particularly frustrated at not being able to get their requirements across. So develop your questioning strategy accordingly – perhaps asking shorter, more focused questions at each stage to relieve the enquirer of having to articulate long, complex sentences in response. Show common courtesy to wheelchair users, who may not be able to get as close to the enquiry desk as they would like when talking to you, or have difficulty retrieving printed documents off shelves for themselves. And don't forget that you can't easily maintain the eye contact that is so essential for ensuring good customer relations if the wheelchair user is seated and you're not.

This is a huge topic, of course, and there's masses of specialist training and advice available which it would be well worth following up, since your job involves such a strong focus on people. But using simple courtesy and common sense can pay dividends too – all with the aim of ensuring that you help your enquirer pursue their journey from question to answer as quickly and efficiently as possible. So . . .

Asking the right questions

Let's get back to the seven enquirers that we considered a moment ago, and their questions. There are ways of dealing with all these. You have to find out what lies behind each of their enquiries by asking questions back, and there are several different questioning techniques that you can employ. This is sometimes rather pretentiously referred to as the reference interview, but that implies an inquisitorial formality about the process that can be off-putting for the enquirer. Much better if it comes out as a structured conversation but – here's the crucial bit – with you in charge.

Who, what, when, where, why, how?

'I keep six honest serving men – they taught me all I knew,' said Rudyard Kipling in the *Just So* stories. To answer any enquiry effectively, you need them too. They are the six questions: Who? What? When? Where? Why? How? It's an excellent formula for kicking off your questioning process. This doesn't mean that you necessarily have to ask them all; your enquirer will fill in some of the blanks relatively unprompted and all you have to do is note that information down. But you should certainly address them all, and try to fill in any gaps with your own questioning.

The first four – Who? What? When? Where? – are pretty obvious and should provide essential information to enable you to answer the enquiry. (On the next page you can see how they work.)

Those are the more straightforward questions to which you need answers. The last two – Why? How? – are a bit more subtle.

First, you can use Why? and How? to seek further details that will help you

Question	What the enquirer's response should tell you
Who?	Who the enquirer is interested in. (This could be a person, an animal, an organization, a civilization, a society, a movement, a concept.) *The answer to the Who? question establishes the character of the subject under discussion. Classically, an enquirer might start by saying: 'Get me everything you've got on x.' If they do pose their question this way, x is probably the answer to the Who? question.*
What?	What activity, aspect, characteristic, quality of that person, animal, organization, etc., they're interested in. *An obvious response from you to a question like that posed above would be: 'Any particular aspect of x?' Whatever the enquirer says in reply will probably be the answer to the What? question.*
When?	Are we dealing with current, recent or historical information? *Very important to establish this, as it's all too easy for you to make erroneous assumptions. You might assume, for example, that a request for information on a historic event or artefact could be satisfied using older sources – until you discover that the enquirer is interested in recently unearthed documents or archaeological finds.*
Where?	Which localities, regions or countries do we have to consider? *Again, don't assume that Where? means 'here'. It's up to you to confirm whether the enquirer is interested only in developments locally or in your own country, or whether they want to take a more international or global approach.*

to understand the subject of the enquiry. There's nothing wrong with you not knowing anything about the enquirer's subject. Why should you? That's not your job. But it is your job to help them with sources and search strategies, and for that you do need to understand at least a little about the enquirer's subject. If you're concerned that you may lose the enquirer's confidence by asking such questions, you can explain, for example, that they will enable you to recognize the terminology involved – so that when you begin searching, or helping the enquirer to search, you'll know when you're on the right lines. If you take that approach, you're immediately moving the conversation back from the enquirer's area of expertise to yours. So . . .

Question	What the enquirer's response should tell you
Why?	Why this person, animal, organization, etc., is acting in this way. *Can provide supplementary information for the Who? question.* Why this activity is being undertaken, and the reasoning behind it. *Can help to make more sense of the What? question.*
How?	How the activity is undertaken or the required results are achieved. *Can help you understand a little more about the answer to the What? question.* How the organization or society or movement operates. *Can help you understand what kind of entity you're dealing with and, possibly, where you might try to find information on it.*

But you can also use the Why? and How? questions to try to understand the enquirer's reasons for asking. This should enable you to ensure that you provide just the right amount of information, fit for purpose, in the most appropriate form. (We'll come back to this towards the end of the chapter.) Like this . . .

Question	What the enquirer's response should tell you
Why?	Why the enquirer is interested in the subject. *Simple curiosity? Personal research? Student project? Work related?*
How?	How the enquirer wants the query handled or the answer delivered. *Just some brief background information? A range of practical solutions? A detailed literature search as a preliminary to major investigation of the subject?*

You wouldn't necessarily always take the questions in this order. (Kipling didn't.) Your enquirer's answers would fill in the blanks for some of them as you went along. Sometimes your questions will seek to elicit more information about the subject the enquirer is interested in, and at other times you will be trying to find out about the enquirer's motives and aspirations. But you certainly shouldn't ask such questions in a direct, unvarnished form. A straight 'What do you want?' or – worse – 'Why do you need to know?' sounds combative and inquisitorial and will almost certainly spoil the temporary but intense relationship that you and the enquirer need to have. What you have to do instead is to weave your questions into the structured conversation that is your goal. So let's move on to . . .

Your interrogation strategy

The first thing to say is that it shouldn't come across as an interrogation – nice cop, nasty cop. Nevertheless an interrogation strategy is what you need and it should allow you to do one or other of two things – funnelling or probing. As we'll see in a moment, it will probably be pretty obvious from the enquirer's first question which strategy you need to start with – although you may need to change your strategy as the conversation develops.

Funnelling focuses the enquirer in from the general to the particular. It's usually the easier of the two techniques to apply because it needn't sound over-inquisitive or threatening. Closed, forced choice and leading questions are all suitable for funnelling operations – although you should bear in mind that each of these techniques carries its own hazards. Forced choice is a particularly effic-ient one. We'll come onto these specific questioning techniques in a moment.

Probing seeks further details from the enquirer when you're not at all clear what they want. But you have to exercise caution and tact when using this technique because it can sound inquisitorial. Open, multiple and hypothetical questions might all help you to probe. On the whole, multiple questions tend to be safest for probing – they don't sound so inquisitorial, they show that you're trying to help and taking the enquiry seriously, and they're more likely to put the enquirer at their ease than on their guard.

Six questioning techniques

We've just mentioned some questioning techniques that might help you achieve your strategy, so let's run through all of them now, and the situations in which you might use them.

Questioning technique	What it can achieve
Open	Could you tell me a little bit more about what you're looking for? *Open questions invite the enquirer to supply further details without you specifying what additional information would be helpful. They can be a good way of putting your enquirer at their ease and getting them to talk. But they don't allow you to structure the conversation in ways that are useful to you.*
Closed	Are you interested in x? *Closed questions force the enquirer to give you a yes/no answer. They can help you to include or eliminate details, and can also be particularly useful at the end of the questioning process, when you want to 'close the deal' with the enquirer by confirming what they want. But if you're going to ask a closed question you need to be pretty sure that you're not inadvertently eliminating aspects of the subject that haven't come up yet.*
Forced choice	Are you more interested in a or b? *Forced choice questions force the enquirer to choose between just two options. It's an immensely powerful questioning technique. First, there are only four possible answers: option 1; option 2; both options; or neither. So immediately you are directing the enquiry in ways that are useful to you. Second, if you ask someone a forced choice question, they're very likely to leap one way or the other – so it can be a great way of unblocking an enquiry where the enquirer is unwilling to talk. True, you have to learn to think quickly to come up with two really useful options – but if you can, they'll probably pay dividends both in terms of what you learn and in demonstrating to the enquirer that you're taking a real interest in their needs.*
Multiple	Are you interested in any of a or b or c or d or e? *Multiple questions offer the enquirer a range of options (more than two) to choose from when you're really not sure what they want and you need to fish for ideas. Of course it's not always easy to think quickly enough to come up with some sensible options – and you might confuse the enquirer by offering too many. So it's worth considering asking a succession of forced choice questions instead, moving from the general to the particular. You could alternatively use a multiple question to explore possible ways of answering the enquiry instead of aspects of the subject – but it's really too early in the process to be thinking about how you might set about providing an answer. For that, we need to wait till Chapter 3.*

Questioning technique	What it can achieve
Leading	So it's information on x that you're interested in, is it? *Leading questions lead the enquirer in the direction of the answer you expect. You should only use them when you're 99% certain you do know what the enquirer wants. They can be dangerous, because they impose your assumptions on the enquirer's request, when you really need to be certain that you haven't made any false assumptions. Like closed questions, though, you can use leading questions to 'close the deal' at the end of the questioning process.*
Hypothetical	If we found you information on x, would that be helpful? *Hypothetical questions attempt to glean further information by putting a hypothetical situation to the enquirer. You're not allowed to ask the forbidden question: 'What do you really want?' That just sounds aggressive and suspicious and sends out the wrong signals to the enquirer. But you can put the same question in a hypothetical form by asking 'What would your ideal answer look like?' Nevertheless hypothetical questions can be dangerous, because they require either you or the enquirer to make something up, taking the situation away from the facts and into the realms of fiction.*

Is there a questioning 'magic bullet'? Probably not. But perhaps **forced choice** questioning comes close because of its diagnostic capabilities. When your optician puts two lenses in front of you in succession and asks: 'Better 1 or 2?' that's a classic forced choice question, enabling the specialist to narrow down the options based on responses from the layperson. But all these questioning techniques have their value at different times. And when you're finally deciding how to set about answering the enquiry or helping the enquirer to answer it – and keep down your own panic at the same time – then the magic bullet is undoubtedly the **hypothetical** question that you ask yourself. (We'll come back to that in Chapter 3.)

Does all this really work?

That's enough of the theory. Let's see how all this might work for the questions to which our enquirers really wanted answers.

Do you have any books on retailing?	Who? What? When? Where? Why? How?	Interrogation strategy	Questioning technique
Yes, plenty – and other kinds of information source as well. Are you interested in retail management, shop design or location, market research, special types of retailer such as food or electrical goods shops – or even one particular retailer?	**What** aspect of retailing are you interested in?	Funnelling	Multiple
Ah, so it is one retailer. Are you looking for financial information or news on the company's activities?	**What** particular activity are you interested in?	Funnelling	Forced choice
So you just need the latest accounts?	**When** are you interested in?	Funnelling	Closed
Just the company's UK business, or does it have worldwide operations as well?	**Where** do we need to consider?	Funnelling	Forced choice

Do you have any books on retailing?	Who? What? When? Where? Why? How?	Interrogation strategy	Questioning technique
Is it detailed data for investment purposes, or just a brief financial profile for information?	**Why** do you need this information?	Funnelling	Forced choice
Do you need to be able to download the figures into a spreadsheet so you manipulate them?	**How** do you want the information presented?	Funnelling	Closed

What the enquirer actually wanted: What is Marks & Spencer's current pre-tax profit? [But you still don't know that yet because you haven't asked which company the enquirer wants.]

Verdict: Enquirers can be extraordinarily secretive about money matters, so it's probably wise to have delayed the crucial question: 'Which retailer is it?' Even so, you haven't wasted your time. There is an enormous amount of business information available and it's easy to bury an enquirer under a deluge of semi-relevant information. So it's worth funnelling to find out precisely what they want without being too specific. By this time, maybe they'll have gained sufficient confidence in you to divulge the name. Or perhaps that's an over-optimistic scenario!

Where do you keep the latest *New Scientist*?	Who? What? When? Where? Why? How?	Interrogation strategy	Questioning technique
The current issue is on the display racks, but we have back issues as well if you're looking for something specific.	**What** are you looking for?	Probing	Open (by implication)
So you'd like to check some back issues as well. How far back would you like to go?	**When** do you think the article appeared?	Funnelling	Open
Are you looking for a particular article that you know appeared in the *New Scientist* or are you just looking for information on a particular topic?	**Why** do you need the *New Scientist* specifically?	Probing	Forced choice
So it's information on radiation risks. If you can't spot the article you remembered from the *New Scientist*, would you like to check elsewhere as well?	**How** do you want to progress your enquiry?	Probing	Closed
Probably the most efficient way to find further information on this topic would be to use our discovery platform for articles that might have appeared in other scientific titles that we have access to. For example, *Nature* covers the same sort of subjects as *New Scientist*.	**Where** else would you like to search?	Probing	Leading (by implication)

What the enquirer actually wanted: I think I saw an article recently about research that's been done into the health effects of radiation, both from artificial and natural sources, and who's doing it. I don't want to appear ignorant so I'm just going to ask for the latest *New Scientist*, which is where I think I saw it. [In fact, the article appeared in *Nature*, and was published months ago.]

Verdict: This may seem like going to enormous lengths to deal with what appears initially to be a very straightforward query. But it turned out not to be straightforward, and your tactful probing may have prevented the enquirer from leaving in a disgruntled mood after failing to find the article in the current *New Scientist*.

I'm looking for information on migration patterns in whales	Who? What? When? Where? Why? How?	Interrogation strategy	Questioning technique
Ah, so we need to be looking in the zoology section?	**Who** are we looking for?	Probing	Closed
Oh, sorry – you mean people moving around Wales?	**What** are they doing?	Probing	Closed
Do you mean things like how they travel to work, or what they do when they move house or where they come from?	**How** are they doing it?	Probing	Multiple
Is it just movements within the country, or from outside as well?	**Where** do we have to consider?	Funnelling	Forced choice
Are you looking just for movements now – or back over a period?	**When** do we have to consider?	Funnelling	Forced choice
Are you looking for information on why people move, or do you just need the figures?	**How** do you want the information presented?	Funnelling	Forced choice

What the enquirer actually wanted: I'm looking for information on migration patterns in Wales.

Verdict: Once you've got over the initial misunderstanding, you should be able to get all the way with this enquiry – it's precise and specific (and we're going to examine the research techniques that lie behind this one in a lot more detail in Chapter 7).

Do you have the *Electrical Register*?	Who? What? When? Where? Why? How?	Interrogation strategy	Questioning technique
I'm sorry, I can't find a directory or website with that name. Is it electricians you're looking for?	**Who** are you looking for?	Probing	Closed
Oh, I beg your pardon, I must have misheard – it's the voters' list you need. The local one or for some other area?	**Where** are you interested in?	Funnelling	Forced choice

Do you have the *Electrical Register*?	Who? What? When? Where? Why? How?	Interrogation strategy	Questioning technique
And I presume you want the current one?	**When** do you want to cover?	Funnelling	Leading
Are you just looking up a specific address, or do you need to browse through?	**What** kind of information do you need to find?	Probing	Forced choice
So you're looking for people with particular surnames. Is this because you're trying to trace someone?	**Why** do you need the information?	Probing	Closed
There might be other kinds of source that could do the job better – websites that can help you trace the origin and distribution of surnames, genealogical sites – even social networking sites. What form would you like the information in?	**How** do you want the enquiry handled?	Probing	Open

What the enquirer actually wanted: Do you have the electoral register? [Yes – but is that really the best source to use for the purpose?]

Verdict: In this instance, we've taken the line of questioning much further than was necessary to answer the enquiry initially posed – even without the misunderstanding. But it does go to show just how much may lie behind even the most apparently simple request. Once you've realized the enquirer's initial mistake, you will need to respond tactfully so as to spare them any embarrassment – and at the very least you will need to confirm that it is the current register for your local area that they want; you shouldn't just assume that it is. But in any case, it's beginning to sound as if the electoral register may not be the most efficient way of meeting the enquirer's needs – so it might be worth taking the questioning even further, while starting to suggest possible solutions at the same time.

I'm trying to find a song called *When I Would Sing Under the Ocean*	Who? What? When? Where? Why? How?	Interrogation strategy	Questioning technique
Right; have you any idea who sings it, or who it's written by?	**Who** are we looking for?	Funnelling	Forced choice
I'm afraid I can't find a song of that title. How did you come to hear of it?	**How** can we take this enquiry forward?	Probing	Open
Oh, you heard it on the radio. Can you remember which station or programme?	**Where** did you hear it?	Funnelling	Open
Was it a pop song or something more traditional?	**When** might it have been written?	Funnelling	Forced choice
Oh, so it was a baritone solo and you think it might have come from an opera or musical?	**What** kind of song was it?	Funnelling	Leading

I'm trying to find a song called *When I Would Sing Under the Ocean*	Who? What? When? Where? Why? How?	Interrogation strategy	Questioning technique
Since it's not showing up in any of our musical sources, perhaps the title's slightly different – so shall we try to think of some other way of identifying it?	**Why** aren't we finding it, when the enquiry seems so straightforward?	Probing	Leading

What the enquirer actually wanted: They still think they're trying to find a song called *When I Would Sing Under the Ocean* – but you by now suspect that the title is probably wrong.

Verdict: At this stage in your questioning, you're not going to find out what you're really supposed to be looking for because the enquirer has almost certainly got the question wrong. As far as you're concerned, you're still looking for a song called *When I Would Sing Under the Ocean* but just not finding it anywhere. However, several things that emerged during your questioning should help you to understand the challenges you face – particularly the fact that the enquirer discovered the title aurally. This should arouse your suspicions; have they misheard it? Meanwhile, though, you do have lots of ideas for places to try: the radio station that played the song; guides to opera and musicals; even asking the enquirer to hum the tune so you can look it up in a dictionary of musical themes or on a music finder website or app.

Have you got any books on Kew Gardens? That's to say, something on the Crystal Palace, if you can manage it. What would be really helpful, actually, would be the index to the *Illustrated London News*. Or, better still, a book on tropical fish.	Who? What? When? Where? Why? How?	Interrogation strategy	Questioning technique
That's a wide range of topics; is there a common factor?	**Who** (or what subject) are you interested in?	Probing	Open
Where do the tropical fish come into it?	**Why** did you mention them?	Funnelling	Open
So it's aquariums. Victorian ones?	**When** would this be?	Funnelling	Closed
And is it particularly London you're interested in?	**Where** are these aquariums?	Funnelling	Closed
So you want to concentrate on one aquarium; which one would that be?	**How** do you want the enquiry to proceed?	Funnelling	Open

What the enquirer actually wanted: I'm doing a project on the Westminster Aquarium.

Verdict: This is probably an over-optimistic scenario. Someone whose requirements are as muddled as this would likely go on muddling for some time before giving you the opportunity to start funnelling. But one advantage that muddlers offer over, say, people who couch their request in very general terms, or those who are being obsessively secretive, is that they do at least give you plenty of clues to work on. And in this instance you also have one huge anomaly which it's really worth focusing on: the fish.

Is it still possible to find information not using the internet?	Who? What? When? Where? Why? How?	Interrogation strategy	Questioning technique
Oh yes – plenty. In books, of course, but also using other printed reference works such as encyclopaedias and directories – and journals and newspapers as well … Of course, if you want to search for something specific, it's much easier if you use subject indexes and other discovery tools. However, these are mostly online and usually delivered over the web.	**How** can I help you?	Probing	Multiple
So you'd really rather just search for yourself through back files of the local newspaper?	**What** sort of information do you need?	Funnelling	Closed
That's fine. Do you know roughly when the event you're looking for happened?	**When** should we start looking?	Funnelling	Closed
I can show you some good scanning techniques to help you find what you need if that would be useful. Could you tell me a subject that you're interested in?	**How** would you like to conduct your search?	Funnelling	Open
So it's questions in the local council about immigration? I know councillors have been discussing it a lot recently. Is there any aspect that particularly interests you?	**What** aspect of the subject should we pursue?	Probing	Closed
Ah, if it's a particular organization you want we might be able to find basic details about it in a printed directory – although to be honest its website is more likely to help you.	**Who** are you looking for?	Funnelling	Forced choice
OK that's fine if you want to stick with the local newspaper for now. If the organization is mentioned, it should be possible to spot its name when scanning.	**How** will you spot the organization?	Funnelling	Closed

Is it still possible to find information not using the internet?	Who? What? When? Where? Why? How?	Interrogation strategy	Questioning technique
And you're also interested in school governorships? Is there a connection with the other issue?	**Why** do you need to know this?	Probing	Closed
So it's a family connection and a question of possible conflict of interest?	**How** are the two issues linked?	Probing	Closed
So in the context of councillors' concerns about immigration, we're looking for something like the rules for school governors?	**How** do you want the subject handled?	Probing	Closed

What the enquirer actually wanted: There's been a report in our local paper about councillors asking questions about the number of immigrants coming into our area. One of those councillors is my brother and I'm a bit concerned because I believe he's involved in something called the Strong & Moral Britain Association, which I think is associated with neo-fascist organizations. Can you confirm this, or let me know where its funding comes from? I really need to know because I'm about to become a governor of a local school with a large number of Asian children – so I'd also like to find out what obligation there is on school governors to declare other interests. But I don't want to approach the school directly about this in case they start asking awkward questions – and I certainly don't want to use the internet to find out, because you never know who's keeping track of your searches. [You don't quite know all of this yet, but you do know enough to get the enquirer started, and you may learn more as you help them to navigate their way through the files of local newspapers.]

Verdict: Despite the length of the interchange, this is a somewhat compressed scenario. It would probably take a lot of very tactful questioning to elicit all the aspects of this complex and sensitive affair. Restricting your questioning initially to things like sources and scanning techniques, as opposed to the specific information required, will probably reassure your enquirer. Then you can use your demonstration of how the source or technique works to find out more about what they actually want – in this case by means of a succession of step-by-step closed questions. At their most basic, closed questions only elicit a yes/no answer – but in this scenario, asking a series of closed questions based on the enquirer's previous responses can gently build on the information they've already been willing to provide and encourage them to disclose more without the process appearing too inquisitorial.

What about hypothetical questions?

If you look back, you'll see that a few of the 'questions' in these little scenarios aren't actually framed as questions at all. But they still invite an answer, nevertheless, and sometimes posing a question as a statement can keep the encounter reassuringly non-inquisitorial. And you may also have spotted that there are no **hypothetical** questions here at all. To be frank, you need to be pretty desperate to ask a hypothetical question – maybe something along the lines of: 'If we found you information on so-and-so, would that be helpful?' To ask a hypothetical you have to make something up, thereby moving the whole process away from the realm of fact and towards fiction. So it's to be avoided if possible. You may sometimes have no choice if you're getting nowhere with any other questioning techniques – but once you've learned what you can from your hypothetical question you should return to the other more facts-based questioning techniques to test what the enquirer told you in their hypothetical answer.

So the message is that you should avoid making hypothetical questions part of your regular interrogation strategy if you possibly can. You've almost certainly had to make heavy use of your analytical thinking skills during the questioning process, and hypothetical questions don't easily support those. It's at the next stage – when you're employing informed creative thinking to work out how to answer the enquiry – that you are definitely going to need the hypothetical questioning technique. But you'll mostly be asking those questions of yourself. We'll return to all this in Chapter 3.

Agreeing the task

As you can see from these examples, some of your questions come out as requests for further information, others as reactions to information received. That's how it usually happens in real life; the responses to either type will help you to fill in more of the blanks. You'll have been taking notes during your structured conversation with the enquirer – won't you? (We'll deal with record keeping in more detail in Chapter 2.) So now is the time to close the deal with the enquirer – confirming what they actually need and then starting to think about what you can do to help.

But just before we do that, let's review where we've got to with each of these enquiries and see what we've achieved . . .

What the enquirer asked	Problem identified	What they actually wanted
Do you have any books on retailing?	Enquirers often ask for something quite **general** when they really need something specific. Didn't take the enquiry at face value but tested to see what lay behind it.	What is Marks & Spencer's current pre-tax profit?
Where do you keep the latest *New Scientist*?	Is this enquirer a bit of a **know-all**? Checked to see what subject they were interested in – and also observed the principle that information people remember seeing almost always comes from further back than they think.	I think I saw an article recently about research that's been done into the health effects of radiation, both from artificial and natural sources, and who's doing it. I don't want to appear ignorant so I'm just going to ask for the latest *New Scientist*, which is where I think I saw it.
I'm looking for information on migration patterns in whales.	'Whales' is a **homophone** – a word that sounds the same as another one although it's spelled differently and has a different meaning. Took a moment or two to resolve this misunderstanding but got there pretty quickly.	I'm looking for information on migration patterns in Wales.
Do you have the *Electrical Register*?	Could have been embarrassing as the enquirer accidentally used a **malapropism** (a word similar to the one intended but meaning something different). A little very mild deceit about mishearing retrieved the situation though.	Do you have the electoral register?
I'm trying to find a song called *When I Would Sing Under the Ocean*.	Can't find any song with that title even though there are plenty of places to look. Because the enquirer heard it on the radio, suspect that this might be a case of **Chinese whispers** (a phrase or sentence that changes through successive mishearings).	[You still don't know what the real song title is. Not knowing the answer is normal in this business – but not knowing the question either is particularly challenging.]
Have you got any books on Kew Gardens? That's to say, something on the Crystal Palace, if you can manage it. What would be really helpful, actually, would be the index to the *Illustrated London News*. Or, better still, a book on tropical fish.	This enquirer has got in a terrible **muddle** explaining what they want. But the whole thing has a Victorian feel about it – and a little bit of lateral thinking about the incongruous fish suggests that an aquarium may be at the heart of it – so tested that with the enquirer.	I'm doing a project on the Westminster Aquarium.

What the enquirer asked	Problem identified	What they actually wanted
Is it still possible to find information not using the internet?	There has to be more to this enquiry than first appears. Sounds as if the enquirer is being pretty **secretive**, but gentle yet persistent questioning gradually elicits the whole story.	Local newspaper . . . council questions on immigrants . . . councillor brother's possible association with neo-fascist organization . . . obligation on enquirer as school governor to declare this? [Though you don't quite know all of this yet.]

So now is the time for you to close the deal with the enquirer. Choosing your words carefully, you need to repeat back to them what you think their real requirements are. Probably the best way to do this is in the form of a **closed** question (hopefully anticipating a 'yes' of agreement from the enquirer) or perhaps a **leading** one, again encouraging the enquirer to agree with you. Something like . . .

- So we just need a single figure – Marks & Spencer's latest pre-tax profit?
- So we're looking for an article on who's doing research into the health risks of artificial and natural radiation, and it's worth searching elsewhere if we don't find the specific article you remember from *New Scientist*?
- So we're looking for figures and commentary on how people have moved into, out of and within Wales between the 2001 and 2011 Censuses and beyond if possible?
- So browsing through the current electoral register for this area might be a useful starting point, but we're also going to locate other sources that may help you to trace the names you're looking for more efficiently?
- So we're looking for a song that's a baritone solo that you probably heard on BBC Radio 2 last Sunday, with a title something like *When I Would Sing Under the Ocean*?
- So we're looking for anything we can find on the Westminster Aquarium, which was demolished some time in the late 19th or early 20th century?
- So our starting point is local newspaper coverage of councillors' concerns over immigration – and especially if there's any mention of one particular organization; and we also need information on the rules affecting school governors' declarations of interest?

Assuming that in each case your enquirer agrees with your diagnosis, you now have an implied contract with them. It may not be legally enforceable, but that's its function nevertheless. If you deviate from it without consulting your enquirer again, then you can no longer guarantee that you're meeting their needs, and you're almost certainly not making the most efficient use of your time either. (We'll come back to occasions when you may need to deviate from the original request in Chapter 5.) And note the use of the word 'we'. It doesn't matter whether you're simply helping your enquirer to locate sources, advising them on using those sources efficiently or undertaking the complete research project yourself – this is your problem now, as well as your enquirer's, and it is only good customer relations to make that clear by involving yourself in it. That includes not simply helping them find the answer, but helping them find it in a form that's useful to them.

Not too little, not too much

Pretty much right up to the end of the 20th century, if you wanted to find something out you usually had to be content with whatever you could glean from a large but strictly limited number of proprietary (and usually charged-for) sources – whether printed, online or published in a portable digital medium such as a CD-ROM. If these didn't yield what you wanted, there wasn't a lot more you could do with documentary sources. You had to either start casting round looking for experts in the field or else give up and be content with at best a second-rate answer.

How things have changed! Almost all those proprietary sources are still there – and usually available in the form of a much wider range of products and media – plus a great many more charged-for services besides. And to all those you have to add information from hundreds of thousands of potentially relevant websites – many of them free – as well as possibly millions of blog posts and billions of comments on social media. When an enquirer asks you 'Get me everything you've got on . . . ' the time is not far off when you're going to be able to do just that. And that's almost certainly too much.

So the last stage in your questioning is to find out more or less how much information your enquirer needs, and of what kind – and this is where your secondary **Why?** and **How?** questions come in: 'Why do you need to know this?' and 'How do you want the enquiry handled or the answer delivered?' If you're actually doing the work on the enquirer's behalf, for instance, you have enough tools to be able to swamp them with information. But you're not helping them if you do that, because they're looking to you not only to find the information they need but also to help them filter it, so that they end up with just enough to do whatever they want to do – no more, no less.

The same applies if you're simply advising – getting a student started on an assignment, for example. They may be doing the actual work, but they still expect you to guide them to the most appropriate sources for their purpose. And you can also seize the opportunity in the process of encouraging them to think critically about the authority and reliability of the different kinds of source they encounter – textbooks, scholarly articles, reports published by specialist organizations, popular journal or news coverage, blog posts (expert or not), social media comment. Authoritative content can sometimes look indistinguishable from the uninformed off-the-cuff variety when viewed on-screen – so you have an important job to do here in helping them to distinguish between what's worth having and what's not. This may be second nature to information professionals – but not always to your enquirers.

So in determining how much information the enquirer wants, and what kind, you could simply ask an open question: 'How much information do you need?' But you might not get a very precise answer; 'Whatever you can find' doesn't really help you very much. Also some enquirers might feel daunted by the task of trying to imagine for themselves what the final answer might look like. That's your job, and we're going to return to it in some detail in Chapter 3. So a multiple question might be better – something like: 'Do you just want a few main points in note form, or a page or so of information, or something like an article, or a complete book?'

This of course assumes that you have a fair idea of the form in which the information is likely to appear. But if it's a highly technical subject, or the enquirer has used terminology that is unfamiliar to you, you might not know what to expect. So a third possibility might be to put the hypothetical question: 'What would your ideal answer look like?' This again puts the onus back on the enquirer, but it may be your only hope if your enquirer really has taken you into totally unfamiliar territory. (Whether or not you ask the *enquirer* this question, it's an absolutely crucial one that you need to ask *yourself* – as we shall see in Chapter 3.)

Information for a purpose

People rarely want information merely to satisfy their curiosity – they almost always need it for a purpose. An **academic** about to embark on a piece of ground-breaking new research may indeed need to know everything that's been discovered on a particular topic – but that almost certainly still only mean everything in the academic and professional literature, and blog posts or other social media comment only from acknowledged specialists in the field. A **practitioner**, with a specific problem to solve, may also want to draw on the same body of specialist literature and seek out comment from the same experts – but may be happy with a good selection of practical solutions to that problem, irrespective of how much more might have been written about it in theory. And yet they may both have started by saying: 'Get me everything you've got on . . . '.

Then there are student assignments. However much you may privately regret a student's lack of curiosity, or deplore the narrow focus of a curriculum that forces this attitude upon them, you have to be realistic about it. You're not helping the hapless student or school child at all if you don't take a pragmatic approach. The fact is that they need enough information to allow them to get a good mark, and once they've got that, they probably can't afford the time to go browsing for more information because they've got other assignments or homework projects also coming up to deadline. So help them find what they want, and then when they've got enough – stop. (But that still doesn't prevent you from developing their information literacy in the process, by encouraging them to appraise what they find critically – see above.)

And of course, you have to know just how much help to give. There's unfortunately no guarantee that different school projects or student assignments undertaken by people at the same stage of educational development necessarily represent tasks of equal difficulty. You can, for example, be faced with two children from the same school class, one of whom wants to do a project on dinosaurs and the other on fourteenth-century Byzantine art. In these circumstances, you clearly need to get the dinosaur child started quickly, and devote the bulk of your attention to the Byzantine one. (We'll look at assessing the ease or difficulty of specific enquiries, and its implications for the management of your time, in Chapter 5.)

Retirement hobbyists, on the other hand, may be operating at the opposite extreme. They're delighted with every additional snippet of detail you can provide, even if they've read it in a dozen other places already. The danger here, of course, is that – in the nicest possible way – they can be terrible time-wasters. Whether you actually get carried along by their enthusiasm, or simply can't shake them off, you have to be systematic about your choice of sources to help them too, and the order of priority in which you suggest them. In both these cases – the student and the hobbyist – the aim is to help your enquirer become self-sufficient as rapidly as possible: to give them something to read, and get them settled down reading it.

Getting answers to these Why? and How? questions may require quite a lot of care on your part. You may need both to probe and funnel to find out whether your enquirer is operating at postgraduate level or starting from a position of total ignorance. No one wants to be thought ignorant, and it's only human nature for people to pretend to greater knowledge than they actually have. So you must use the answers to your Who? What? When? Where? Why? How? questions to judge how much your enquirer knows already. Again, this determines the types of source you use or recommend. A layperson asking about varicose veins may just want a medical dictionary, a home health guide or a health advice web page – but a nursing student probably wants articles from the clinical press. An enquirer who asks you for textbooks about anatomy may be a paramedic studying fractures, but may equally be an art student studying life drawing.

Finding out how long you've got

Finally, you have to agree a deadline. Often, this will be 'now'. The enquirer will be standing there, and they'll want you to point them in the right direction straight away. But if the enquiry has come in by phone, e-mail or text, or if the enquirer is going to leave now and let you get on with it, you need to be quite clear when they need the answer. So don't take 'As soon as possible' or 'It's urgent' for an answer. 'As soon as possible' could mean next year from your point of view, and urgency can be measured in minutes or days. So politely pin your enquirer down to a date, and a time too if the deadline is tight.

Admittedly this isn't always easy when you're dealing with a senior colleague in your organization or a peppery academic in your college, or even sometimes an impatient and intimidating member of the public. So be prepared to explain why you need to agree a firm deadline: so that you can provide as full a response as is feasible within the timescale. And if you think that timescale is unrealistically short, try not to say: 'Can't be done'. Keep it positive. Perhaps explain that you will be able to provide a rough-and-ready answer in that time, but might be able to improve on it if the enquirer is able to extend the deadline. Put like that, you'll find more often than not that they are able to give you more time. (We'll deal with meeting deadlines in Chapter 5.)

Coming next – when the enquirer's not there . . .

We've discovered that plenty can go wrong with even the apparently simplest of enquiries. We've found out a bit about how to avoid some of these pitfalls and learned that good customer care is an essential part of the process. But that's when you actually have the enquirer standing in front of you. When the enquirer's at the other end of the phone, e-mailing or texting in, or communicating using social media, even more things can go wrong and maintaining good customer relations becomes more vital still. So in Chapter 2, we'll look at how we need to think empathetically when dealing with enquirers remotely.

To recap . . .

- **Beware of the pitfalls presented by enquiries that seem too general, know-all enquirers, homophones, malapropisms, Chinese whispers, muddlers and the obsessively secretive.**
- **Look for answers to the questions Who? What? When? Where? Why? How?**
- **Be ready to funnel or probe as appropriate, and employ open, closed, forced choice, multiple, leading or hypothetical questions.**
- **Reach firm agreement about what you will do for the enquirer, and in how much detail.**
- **Make sure you agree a clear deadline for the work too.**
- **Use your analytical thinking skills to achieve all this.**

CHAPTER 2

Why remote enquiry handling is different

Anticipating problems by thinking empathetically

In this chapter you'll find out how to:

- **deal with enquiries that come in via a voice- or text-based medium**
- **avoid even more misunderstandings**
- **get into the habit of good record keeping**
- **keep your enquirer on-side by thinking empathetically.**

'Please listen carefully to the following three options: To annoy the customer, press 1; to waste everybody's time, press 2; to lose business, press 3.'

Up to now we've been assuming that your encounter with the enquirer has been face to face; we've learned quite a bit about what can go wrong if you don't anticipate potential misunderstandings and be ready to deal with them before they happen. But at least you've had plenty of other clues – besides what you and the enquirer actually say to one another – to reinforce your suspicion that things might be going wrong.

You might detect a pained expression flitting across the enquirer's face as they realize that they're not getting their needs across. They might be drumming their fingers with impatience at the lack of progress, or standing with their arms akimbo as if to demand an explanation. Or they might be avoiding eye contact with you – indicating, perhaps, that they have something to hide or, worse, that they don't have confidence in your ability to help them.

When you observe 'tells' like this, that does at least give you an opportunity to take remedial action. But when you can't see, and sometimes can't even hear, your enquirer, you have none of these clues to draw upon, and that means that even more things can go wrong than we encountered in Chapter 1.

As the quote at the start of this chapter indicates, remote contact centres tend to have a pretty terrible reputation. But when you do encounter a good one, you'll find it leads the way in high-quality customer service. That lesson applies just as much to information services as it does to those provided by banks, travel firms or IT helpdesks. Like them or loathe them, people are expecting more and more of the services they need to be delivered remotely.

They may be students who want instant guidance from their university resource centre before embarking on their own literature search online. They could be colleagues or superiors in some distant office in your organization for whom time is money. Or they might be users who simply want to check that there's going to be something useful for them to look at before they come into their local library. Whatever their needs, you must be ready to satisfy them whether they choose to communicate by phone, e-mail, text or messaging.

Once again, there's a formal phrase that pulls all of these practices together: virtual reference. It can encompass videoconferencing and Voice Over Internet Protocol (VOIP) as well as things like phone, e-mail and texting. But the actual communication medium, and the technology that enables it, are less important than the tactics you deploy when using that medium to ensure that your relationship with the enquirer runs smoothly. So before we continue, let's be quite clear about the kinds of media we're talking about. This chapter is concerned with enquiries that require you to use **interactive one-to-one remote communication media** – including . . .

Voice-based (where you and the enquirer can hear and possibly see each other)	Landline telephone Mobile telephone Voice Over Internet Protocol (VOIP) Teleconferencing *All whether standalone or offered as part of a broader social media package*
Text-based (can include still or moving images as well depending on the technology, but not audible contact)	E-mail Short Message Service (SMS – i.e. texting) Instant messaging Chat Fax (if still used) *Again whether standalone or offered as part of a broader social media package*

Before we continue, just a quick word about video communication technology – adding visual contact to a voice-based medium, using either a webcam or teleconferencing facilities. Obviously this overcomes some of the difficulties associated with voice-based media, perhaps making the experience a little more like face to face. But no matter how high-quality the screen image, the resolution still won't compare with face to face, and you're quite likely to miss nuances of expression that you would probably pick up if you and the enquirer were actually together. The image is almost certain to be smaller than real life too, and the field of vision will be limited – so your enquirer wouldn't for example be able to follow you with their eyes if you turned away to look something up. There's no doubt that video could add value to the experience for both of you, but it probably still wouldn't compare with face to face. It occupies a rather awkward halfway house between face to face and remote, in fact.

For brevity and clarity's sake, we're going to refer to the other two types of medium that we are going to consider in this chapter as either 'voice-based' or 'text-based', and use the term 'remote' when we could mean either type or both. However, we may use words like 'phone' or 'e-mail' when illustrating with examples. The crucial thing, though, is that it's all about being aware that when you can't see or hear each other you're deprived of most of the clues that we take for granted when dealing with people face to face. This means that you really need to empathize with the enquirer to avoid things going wrong – another thinking skill that comes with experience.

Can't see, can't hear – the risk of misunderstanding, even offence

Let's get the bad news out of the way first. All sorts of extra things can go wrong when you're dealing with enquirers remotely, and here are some of the reasons why . . .

Opening hours

Face to face: When they have to come to your building to use your services, users do generally appreciate that you have opening hours and other times when you're closed, and they'll expect to see a notice outside saying what those times are.

Remote: As far as remote customers are concerned, you're never closed. After all, you're not just providing remote services for their convenience; it's also benefitting you in terms of saved premises costs – so the least you can do in return is be open all hours. You may not actually like the idea of working

24 hours a day, but you need to be aware that that may be what your enquirer expects.

Response time

Face to face: When the enquirer's actually with you, they can see you're working and are generally prepared to wait a bit while you deal with people ahead of them in the queue.

Remote: When they can't see that you're working hard – either on their enquiry or somebody else's while they wait their turn – there's a tendency for remote enquirers to assume that you're on a permanent tea break, from the moment you hang up the phone after taking their enquiry to the time you do finally return their call. And that's not even considering the time they may have spent waiting to get through to you in the first place – so you might find you have a disgruntled customer on your hands before you even start.

Customer loyalty

Face to face: If an enquirer has bothered to make the journey to your premises in the first place, they're likely to stick with you even if you're having difficulty satisfying their requirements. They've already invested time in coming to see you, and they'll have to use up even more time if they decide to give up on you and travel somewhere else – with no guarantee of faring any better when they do.

Remote: It may only have taken a few minutes for the customer to put their enquiry into an e-mail, or to phone or text you – so if they decide they're not getting good service, it's only going to take a few minutes more to phone somewhere else instead or click on a different link. Why should they wait if they're not happy?

Service quality

Face to face: Hopefully, an enquirer should get service of the same high quality wherever they choose to go – and that includes being given an answer of comparable quality no matter who they ask. But if they feel that they're not getting good service, it's still probably less hassle to stay where they are and persevere, rather than perhaps waste time going elsewhere in search of a better answer.

Remote: If an enquirer doesn't like the answer you've provided, and feels they can get a better one elsewhere, it doesn't matter how hard you've worked on their behalf. It's so easy and quick for them to try somewhere else that they'll quite likely do just that.

Searching time and effort

Face to face: If you have the enquirer with you, you can give them some initial advice and then leave them browsing print materials or looking through search results while you deal with somebody else. Your enquirer can see that you're not slacking, and hopefully also understands that they can ask you for further help whenever they need it.

Remote: If you're dealing with an enquiry that has come in by voice- or text-based media, you really have to do all the searching, and the selection and rejection of possible sources, on the enquirer's behalf. It's no good telling the enquirer 'Oh, you'll have to come in', because what's the point of offering a remote service if they have to do that? Instead, you'll probably have to do a lot more work on the enquirer's behalf, and they'll likely have done the simple searching themselves already.

Cross-selling and up-selling

Quick explanation of these two terms first of all. **Cross-selling** is when you ask for one thing and the provider tries to sell you something else of comparable value at the same time. You might go into your local coffee shop just to buy a pastry, and the server asks: 'Would you like a drink with that?' That's cross-selling. **Up-selling** is when you've bought something of a certain value and the provider tries to sell you something of higher value. They might be trying to persuade you to come off a pay-as-you-go tariff on your mobile phone, for example, and go onto a longer-term subscription plan instead. If they succeed in persuading you to change, that's up-selling.

Now you may think that none of this applies to you, running an information service. You're not actually selling anything, and you've got a captive market in any case. You'd probably be wrong on both counts.

First, even if no money changes hands with each enquiry, someone's still paying you to provide the service you do. It could be a student paying high tuition fees (and probably incurring long-term debt in the process), a colleague or superior who may be inclined to see the corporate information unit as an overhead rather than a profit centre, or simply a member of the public who pays their local taxes. Whichever it is, it's your enquirer who pays in the end – and quite reasonably expects value for money.

And you haven't got a captive market any more either, even if you ever did. Your student can use a social network to ask one of their peers; your colleague or superior can use the professional association of which they're a member; and your member of the public can simply go on the web.

So with that possible misconception out of the way . . .

Face to face: Someone who visits your premises in person can browse around while they're waiting for a member of staff to help them, and perhaps find the very thing they need by serendipity – maybe even something better than you thought to offer them.

Remote: Apart from browsing through whatever you provide on your website, a remote enquirer is entirely in your hands when it comes to ideas for places to look. If they've already looked on the web unsuccessfully, it's up to you to come up with higher-value sources to try, and to contribute your own expertise as a professional searcher. Not to mention seizing any opportunity you can to persuade your student to come on a library induction course, your colleague or superior to sign up for your current awareness service, or your member of the public to attend a local event that relates to their interests.

Non-verbal clues

Face to face: As the opening scenario of this chapter suggests, we get most of the clues as to how our brief but intense relationship with the enquirer is going not from the words they use but from how they appear to be reacting. It's probably not wise to try to put actual figures on it, but as a general rule it's safe to assume that we gain only a fraction of the clues we need from what the enquirer actually says, and rather more from how they say it. If you doubt this, just repeat a simple sentence over and over – 'I hope you can help me', for example – and try putting the emphasis on each word in turn. You'll probably be astonished at how your perception of the mood of the enquirer changes each time.

However, it's generally agreed that we can learn most of all about how the enquirer's feeling – and take remedial action where necessary – not from what they say or how they say it but from their body language, facial expression and eye contact. So when you're dealing with an enquirer face to face, don't just focus on your workstation or keep your nose buried in your notes. Look at them as much as possible; it will tell you a lot.

Remote: With voice-based media, you can hear what your enquirer is saying and the tone of voice they're using, but you can't see if they're secretly getting impatient or losing confidence in you. They may sound as if they're being patient, but may actually be silently rolling their eyes in exasperation. And if it's a text-based medium, you don't even have tone of voice to go on. Even if the words look restrained and polite, you have no idea what emphasis the enquirer is putting on them – and as we've already seen, that emphasis can change the character of a message dramatically.

And last of all . . .

Keeping in touch

Face to face: Hopefully this is fairly straightforward when the enquirer is actually on the premises. If they're working in your library or information unit, you can go back to them over and over again to support them as their researches proceed – or, if they're in another office in the building, a quick internal phone call may be sufficient to resolve any queries.

Remote: The plethora of available remote communication media, and the services providing access to them, continues to grow inexorably. Corporate consolidation may eventually render this less of a challenge, but for the moment reaching agreement with the enquirer over the chosen media you will use to keep in touch is essential. Evidence suggests that the time is fast approaching when the majority of people will be using mobile devices – smartphones or tablet computers – to communicate, rather than desktop computers or fixed-line phones. The change is affecting the dynamics of enquiry answering and we must be ready for it.

Keeping your remote enquirer on-side

Right – that's the bad news dealt with. Now we need to consider how to avoid all these potential pitfalls.

The first thing to say is that everything we learned in Chapter 1 applies here too, only even more so. Your initial interrogation strategy – whether to funnel or probe – and the questioning techniques you use are both essential, because with a remote enquirer you have if anything even less time and opportunity to discover what they really want.

Why? Because unless it's a very straightforward enquiry, you're quite likely to need to take the enquirer's details and then promise to get back to them using whatever medium you agree upon. That means that you absolutely must gather all the information you need during that first phone call or in the first rapid exchange of e-mails or texts.

When the enquirer is physically with you, you do have the opportunity to ask further questions that you may not have thought of at the beginning without risking their becoming too impatient, because they can see you're working hard on their behalf. But when the enquirer is somewhere else, and perhaps wondering what on earth you're doing all this time, each time you contact them again remotely they're going to think you're coming back with the answer at last. They're going to become understandably more and more impatient if you need to ask yet another question that you should have thought to ask in the first place. So your Who? What? When? Where? Why? How?, plus your discussion of what they need the information for, how much detail they want and how they want the answer delivered – and your agreement on a deadline for the job, are as vital as ever.

And to all the risks of misunderstanding that we looked at in Chapter 1, you have to add things like noisy phone connections, the signal breaking up, the call being dropped because the enquirer's train has just gone into a tunnel, any of which can either add to the risk of mishearing, or interrupt your thought processes. And when it comes to text-based media, you have the additional hazard of misleading typos. If someone e-mails or texts you asking how they can become a qualified diver in France, how are you to know that they actually mean a qualified *driver* – unless you ask a supplementary question? And when you do think to ask it, how can you be sure that your message doesn't come across as flippant or patronizing?

So some thoughts about remote enquiry etiquette . . .

When the phone rings . . .

This may seem counter-intuitive, but don't snatch it up immediately. (Of course the other principle applies too: don't let it ring interminably.) Even though they've initiated the call, an enquirer often uses the ringing time to gather their thoughts. They may even be taking the pessimistic, but often all too justified, view that their call is *unlikely* to be answered with any degree of promptitude, so they might as well put the ringing time to good use by thinking what they're going to say.

So if you do snatch the phone up before it's even had time to finish its first ring, you'll quite possibly be dealing with a surprised and confused enquirer who doesn't actually hear the first few words you say and has to ask you to repeat them. If you let the phone ring two or three times before picking it up, you're much more likely to have a composed and attentive enquirer on your hands.

Your phone style

When you answer the phone, what are you going to say? Do you start with 'Good morning', 'Hello' or 'Hi'? Do you say the full name of your organization or just use its abbreviation or acronym and hope that the caller will know they've come through to the right place? Remember, you can't see if your enquirer looks stiff and formal, or relaxed and laid-back. So you need to agree (with your team or management if appropriate) what form of initial greeting you'll use, neither too formal nor too informal. At this point, what you say on the phone *is* your organization's branding, just as much as its signage, stationery, publicity material and website are.

But that doesn't mean reading from a script. That's almost certain to sound forced and robotic, and it also sends out the message that the enquirer's requirements are going to have to match your procedures, instead of you being flexible in meeting the enquirer's needs. Using a script can also put you at a disadvantage, because you have to stick to the prescribed words while the enquirer can say anything they like in response, forcing you to fight with one hand tied behind your back. Remember, this is supposed to be a structured conversation, but with you (tactfully) in charge.

Sometimes you do need to include specific information for legal purposes – a disclaimer saying that you're not qualified to give legal or medical advice, a reassurance that the enquiry will be dealt with in confidence, or a warning that the call may be recorded for training purposes. Again, if at all possible, it's best not to have to read this from a script; try to get clearance to use your own commonsense form of words, based on clear guidelines about the information that you have to convey.

Speaking speed and clarity

Your enquirer is going to need a little more time to adjust to your voice, your accent and what you're saying when on the phone – and they may be taking notes too. With no visual signals, the voice is all you and the enquirer have, so what you say and how you say it become all the more important. So speak at a slightly steadier pace than you would perhaps need to face to face. Spoken news reporters often use a rule of thumb of three words a second. It's slightly slower than normal conversation, but it's not as slow as dictation speed, and a good benchmark to adopt, with practice.

And – just in case you're worrying – this has nothing to do with your accent. Your accent is special, it's your precious legacy, it's what makes you 'you'. So celebrate your accent – but still make sure you speak steadily and clearly.

International callers and enquirers not using their first language

Which brings us on neatly to enquirers and *their* accents. First, if you think someone may be putting in a voice call from abroad, and perhaps incurring time costs, it might be courteous to help keep their costs down by offering to continue the conversation using a text-based medium. Or if you use Voice Over Internet Protocol (VOIP) yourself, you could offer to call them back using that usually cheaper, if not actually free, medium. If you do suggest this, and they agree, then it's pretty essential to resume the conversation in the new medium more or less straight away. If you don't, the enquirer may think you're just fobbing them off. One incidental benefit of changing from a voice- to a text-based medium is that it may make it easier to understand what the enquirer wants if they have a strong accent on the phone. But that shouldn't be a reason for suggesting continuing the conversation in a text-based medium; it's a bonus.

If you are having difficulty understanding someone's accent on the phone it can be a real challenge, but there are some things you can do about it nevertheless. Think carefully, for example, about the kinds of questions you use. Closed and forced choice questions, for example, require the enquirer to respond to your suggestions rather than having to frame sentences and recall vocabulary for themselves. However, in order to ask such questions you need to have listened to at least some of the enquirer's requirements to begin with.

If you try all this and still have problems understanding, risking wasting the enquirer's time as a result, you could perhaps claim that the connection is noisy, or that you're having difficulty hearing. It has to be said that this isn't a particularly ethical approach if it's not true, but it may be justified if the outcome is that you're able to start helping the enquirer while keeping the relationship positive.

And finally, show the enquirer some courtesy yourself. As well as speaking more steadily, try to use short sentences with few subordinate clauses. But don't fall into the trap of using excessively simple words, and certainly don't shout – that's just patronizing. (Go back to Chapter 1 for a recap on other issues associated with understanding and responding to voices and accents.)

Laconic or loquacious enquirers

Even if you and your enquirer do share a native language, that still doesn't necessarily mean that they're going to make their wishes clear and unambiguous. Some people may provide very clipped and unhelpful answers over the phone, followed by an awkward silence while you decide how to respond (and silences on the phone seem much longer than silences face to face). Others might ramble on without giving you an opportunity to ask supplementary questions because they're unable to see any gestures that might indicate that you would like to intervene.

Once again, you can deploy different questioning techniques to meet each situation. For laconic enquirers, open questions might encourage them to expand on their requirements, or multiple questions might induce them to opt for one or more choices. Loquacious enquirers might be brought to heel with closed or forced choice questions to help them focus.

Fielding complaints

It's a depressing thing to have to think about, but there's always the possibility that the next call you take is going to be a complaint. There is even a suggestion that people who initially enquired by e-mail will subsequently complain by phone – but whether that's true or not, the fact is that you get none of the clues that someone's unhappy with your service before the phone rings and they start complaining at you.

When you're dealing with a complainer face to face, you're quite likely to have seen them approach you with a determined expression and tension in their body, so you do at least have a second or two to get into complaint-deflection mode. But when you pick up the phone, it comes at you without warning.

One common complaint comes from the caller who claims they were speaking to someone but got cut off. This is a tricky one; it may be true or it may be a ploy. Obviously you can use some of the questioning techniques we discussed in Chapter 1 to try to discover who they might have been speaking to before and hopefully put them back to that person. But if that's not possible it means that the complainer becomes your responsibility, and it's sensible customer relations to give them some sort of priority, if only for the sake of sending them away placated instead of disgruntled.

But complaints can actually come in all manner of guises. So the first piece of advice is: always assume that the next call is going to be a complaint. Although this may sound a dismal approach to adopt, the reality is that most of your calls are not going to be complaints (unless you're very unlucky or your organization has done something to annoy a lot of people), so immediately you can start off feeling happier about things than you did before you picked up. And if you do find yourself having to calm an irate caller or stand up to someone who's trying to bully you over the phone, here are a couple of things you can try.

If you judge that the complaint is justified, and you want to placate the enquirer and reassure them that you will put things right, try smiling. It can subtly change the character of your voice and perhaps ease the situation. This doesn't mean a grin suggesting that you're not taking the complaint seriously, or a rictus implying that you're scared stiff; just do what common sense would suggest you do if the complainer were standing in front of you and you may well find that you can defuse the situation as a result.

If you feel you're being browbeaten with an unjustified complaint, or if you think the complaint is justified but the enquirer is overreacting or even bullying, that can be pretty intimidating. You may relapse into confusion, tempting the complainer to press home their advantage, or you may lose your cool, with potentially disastrous consequences for your customer relations. So you could try continuing the conversation standing up. Your enquirer can't see that you've stood up and so can't regard it as provocative, but it can sometimes give you the extra confidence you need to regain the situation. Of course it may look odd to those around you but that doesn't matter; it's the person at the other end of the phone you have to be concerned with.

Now a quick health warning: these techniques don't work for everybody. So just try them if you feel inclined and see if they work for you. One thing you must do, though, is take phone complaints if anything more seriously than you would complaints delivered in person. You've no idea how long the person at the other end has had to get worked up about it, and you can't use your facial expression or body language to show that you're empathizing. Before social media, it used to be that people who felt they'd had bad service tended to tell three times as many people as those who'd had good service. Nowadays they're more likely to go online and sound off to everyone in their social media circle – potentially hundreds of people. They'll probably really embellish the story too. Mistakes sometimes get made, but it's how you rectify them that matters.

So – while we're on the subject of complainers, whether encountered face to face or remotely – just a few quick tips on ways to deal with them. First – empathize but stand your ground. Acknowledge that they have a grievance (whether justified or not) but don't bend the rules just because the customer is cross. If something has gone wrong, try to deliver any good news first – for example, how you intend to rectify the situation; that will hopefully soften the blow of any bad news you have to give – such as why you can't change the rules to suit the customer's convenience. If you need to refer a complainant on to a colleague, warn the colleague first if you can. And if you really are in the wrong, don't try to bluff your way out of it; confess, apologize and be ready to come up immediately with a possible solution.

Finally on complaints, remember that if you're responding in writing you'll need to be careful about how you word your message. You have no control over where the recipient lays the stress on the words you use, and they could interpret what you thought was a perfectly reasonable explanation as being bureaucratic or obstructive. Which leads us neatly on to . . .

Responding to text-based messages

Just as you should never take an oral enquiry at face value (whether face to face or by phone) so you should treat text-based enquiries with caution too. Just because the act of composing a written message gives the enquirer the opportunity to state their requirements succinctly and comprehensively, that doesn't mean that they'll actually do so. (Remember the 'diver' versus 'driver' incident above.) So the all-important supplementary question that we looked at in Chapter 1 is no less crucial here.

Responding to a text-based message with a supplementary question has another benefit too: It reassures the enquirer that you've received their enquiry and are working on it. Because it's less instantly interactive than voice-based communication, sending a text-based message – e-mail, SMS, chat – is bit of an act of faith for the enquirer. They've no idea that it hasn't just gone into a void until you respond.

And you don't necessarily have to respond using the same medium either.

If you've received an enquiry by text or e-mail, a quick phone call may be a more efficient way of obtaining the further information you need, and can also demonstrate to the enquirer that you're treating their request with urgency. But if you do decide, for example, to respond to an e-mail with an e-mail, you need to be ready for perhaps several further e-mail exchanges before you can 'close the deal' on the work to be done.

It's better if this exchange can happen fairly rapidly, so it may be worth delaying your initial e-mail (or SMS) response until you know you have the time to handle several back-and-forth communications in rapid succession. There's no guarantee that it will work out like that of course – your enquirer may have gone into a meeting or lecture immediately after sending their enquiry – but it's wise to be able to make yourself available in case they do respond quickly.

Enquiries received by SMS should be prime candidates for a response using a different medium. As we saw in Chapter 1, the apparently briefest and simplest of requests can conceal a great deal more detail that requires investigation by you, and the cramped and tiny screen of even the most generously proportioned phone is probably not the best display device to use. So perhaps you could text back a quick holding response and ask if you can either talk directly or (if there's time) get some further background by e-mail.

Then there's the issue of how you respond to messages that are full of contractions (e.g. 'cul8r', 'lol') and rounded off with a smiley face. Do you reciprocate, risking misunderstandings if your own contractions aren't self-evident? Or do you keep it formal, with the danger that the enquirer will dismiss you as stuffy and devalue the help you might have been able to offer as a result? No answers to such dilemmas yet, but we will return to them when we look at how you can present your answer well, in Chapter 6.

The same principle applies the other way around, too. If for example you receive an enquiry by phone, an e-mail response outlining what you've agreed to do can both reassure the enquirer and also provide the start of an audit trail. This could be highly desirable if you have to hand the enquiry on to a colleague, which is something that we'll be looking at in the next section.

Keeping good records

We touched on record keeping in Chapter 1. We looked at how your note taking during the initial dialogue with the enquirer should enable you to confirm exactly what you intend to do to help them, with no misunderstandings – providing neither too little information nor too much. We've also seen how important it is to agree an unambiguous deadline for the work.

Record keeping matters at all times, not just to enable you to keep track of the progress of enquiries but also to provide longer-term evidence of the value of the service you provide. However, it's probably true to say that when you have your enquirer physically with you you're less likely to lose track of them or forget what you were doing for them, so the need for a really detailed record of the enquiry may not be quite so crucial. But when your enquirer isn't there at all, then a good record becomes absolutely essential.

As we've already seen earlier in this chapter, you can't keep going back to your remote enquirer to ask supplementary questions. Each time you do so they'll assume you're going to provide the answer, so they'll be understandably peeved if it's just another question about something you forgot. You'll also need at least two methods of communicating with them – phone and e-mail for example – because if you don't you can be sure that the moment you need to contact them urgently their phone will be out of range or their laptop battery will be flat.

So it really helps to use enquiry recording procedures that cover everything you might need to ask. What kind of procedures, using what kind of tool? That's for you or your management to decide, and we'll come back to some enquiry tracking packages that you could use in Chapter 8 on Choosing Your Toolkit. But there are some other things we need to consider first.

Privacy

You're almost certainly going to record personal information about your enquirer – name, contact details, what they want and why. So your organization needs to be registered for data protection, detailing the specific purpose for which you need to record and hold the information that you use to identify the enquirer. The details may vary from jurisdiction to jurisdiction, but your organization is likely to be required to guarantee (among other things) that it will only use the information for the purpose for which it has been collected, that it will not collect any more information than is necessary, and that it will keep it for no longer than it needs to.

This can raise some tricky issues. How much is enough information for the purpose, when you may have had to delve into the enquirer's motives for asking to ensure that you can provide an answer appropriate to their needs?

What does keeping the record only for as long as necessary mean? Just till the initial enquiry is completed? The enquirer may want to come back later asking you to take the investigation further – and may be relying on you to have kept a record of what you've done so far. And you'll certainly want to use the results of completed enquiries to add to your performance data and perhaps for your own know-how or Frequently Asked Question (FAQ) files.

Whatever way you (or your management) has resolved these issues, you may need to reassure your enquirer that you are permitted to record personal data for enquiry-answering purposes, and that you will (of course) treat their request in confidence.

Audit trail and ownership

At the very least, you'll need to ensure that you have enough detail to enable you to report back to the enquirer on how you tackled the task and what progress you made. When the enquirer isn't actually with you, it may not be so easy to keep checking back with them as and when you find things – so you need a good research record to present to them at the end if necessary. Equally crucially, you may need to hand the enquiry over to a colleague, in which case you have to make sure that your colleague doesn't waste time by going over sources and search strategies that you've tried already.

At every stage in its life, too, someone needs to 'own' the enquiry. When you first take it, and agree the task with the enquirer, that someone is you. It's perfectly all right to transfer that ownership to someone else – someone taking over from your shift, for example, or a subject specialist better qualified to answer – but the buck always has to stop with someone and that someone needs to be on the record.

What to record . . .

Every information service's needs are different, so the decision on exactly what to record has to be yours (or your manager's). But here's a checklist of items to consider – whether you're developing your own system in-house (using standard database software for instance) or evaluating one or more of the available enquiry tracking tools (e.g. those listed in Chapter 8):

Section	Record (or consider recording) . . .
The enquirer	Name Organization Address Postcode *(worth recording this in a separate field in case you ever want to do market research based on your enquirers' location)* Landline phone Mobile VOIP identifier E-mail Instant messaging or chat Fax *(unlikely these days – but you never know)* Special contact instructions *(e.g. try mobile first, e-mail second; call between specific times; don't mention subject of enquiry to whoever picks up the phone)* [Try to get at least two contact points in case the preferred one isn't working when you need to report back and the deadline is looming. If you're taking enquiries using a web form, make sure that the contact information goes into a 'compulsory' field, which the enquirer has to fill in before the enquiry will be accepted.]
The enquiry	Narrative description *(as much detail as necessary)* Deadline *(date and – if necessary – time)* Enquiry taken by . . . Enquiry transferred to . . . *(there could be several of these)*
Enquiry analysis	Who? What? When? Where? Why? How? *(as discussed in Chapter 1)* What will the final answer look like? *(we'll deal with this in Chapter 3)* Focus, dynamism, complexity, viability *(more on this in Chapter 3 too)* Who really needs to know this? *(explained in Chapter 5)*
Search strategy	Root terms, broader terms, narrower terms, related terms *(more on these in Chapter 4)* Search methodology *(how you chose and logically linked your search terms – again, more on this in Chapter 4)* Sources tried *(the list of Starter Sources in Chapter 8 may help you here)* Search results *(what you found – and where)* The answer *(we'll deal with how you might present it to the enquirer in Chapter 6, and with turning search results into a narrative research report in Chapter 7)*
Sign-off	Who completed the enquiry Who delivered the answer *(may not be the same person)* Degree of success in answering it: complete; partial; compromise How satisfied the enquirer was *(not necessarily the same as how successful you were in answering it)* If the enquiry was referred to someone else – whether within your organization or outside it – then who? How long it took to answer *(hours and minutes)* When completed *(date and time)* Delivered on time? If not, why not? Follow-up actions *(add new information to FAQs, Know-How files or Starter Sources; consider newly discovered sources or services for purchase or subscription)* [There's much more on sign-off activities in Chapter 6.]

This may seem like an awful lot to record. But if answering information enquiries on behalf of your users – in a public reference library or as a researcher working for an organization – is part of your job, it's difficult to see how you can avoid going through each of these stages. There may be a case for recording less if you're working in a university, college or school library, where it's the students who are supposed to be doing the research and not you. But even here, demonstrating good research practice can be a crucial part of your learning support role, and keeping a record of what you've advised can both help future students and demonstrate to the authorities the value of the contribution the library makes.

Whatever your view on this, the enquirer and enquiry details are essential, and you'd be recording these during the initial dialogue anyway. The same probably goes for the Who? What? When? Where? Why? How?

The other elements of the enquiry analysis are pretty essential, too, if you're actually doing the research on the enquirer's behalf, as we'll discover in later chapters, and you'll need to record them as you go along. It's only sensible to record the stages in your search strategy, to ensure you don't accidentally go over the same ground twice – and it's essential to do so if you have to hand the enquiry to someone else half-finished. And as for the sign-off details – well, they provide crucial performance data that you may depend on when bidding for next year's funding (or even staving off cuts) and they can also help you deliver a more efficient, customer-focused service next time. All in all, then, there isn't much you can really afford to leave out.

. . . and how to record it

Well, you could always use the tried and tested paper enquiry form – but this does seem to be missing an awful lot of tricks. You're dependent on an increasingly dog-eared piece of paper that could get mislaid at any stage in the process – especially if you transfer the enquiry to someone else – in which case your audit trail is compromised. And, crucially, gathering performance data from a stack of paper forms is an incredibly labour-intensive operation. So you could try creating a form tailor-made for you, using a standard database or spreadsheet package. However, there are several purpose-built packages available that specifically enable you to keep track of progress on enquiries – whether face to face or remote. We've listed some in Chapter 8 on Choosing Your Toolkit.

Coming next – avoiding panic, thinking on your feet

Now at last you have all the information you need to actually start hunting for the answer. But where are you going to look? This is often the time when your mind goes blank and you start to panic. But there are techniques you can use to help you see your way from mystery to potential solution, and deal with your panic at the same time. So in Chapter 3 we'll look at how to get started on answering your enquiry and learn about deploying another thinking skill: thinking imaginatively.

To recap . . .

- **With remote enquiries, you're deprived of most of the clues we take for granted when dealing with people face to face.**
- **The risk of misunderstanding – even offence – is high.**
- **Use good customer service techniques to keep your enquirer on-side.**
- **Good record keeping is essential when your enquirer is somewhere else.**
- **Your empathetic thinking skills are crucial.**

CHAPTER 3

Getting started

Dealing with the panic by thinking imaginatively

In this chapter you'll find out how to:

- **imagine what the final answer will look like**
- **decide what kinds of source will provide that answer**
- **determine the best delivery medium to use**
- **start identifying actual sources**
- **exercise your imaginative thinking skills.**

Fear of the unknown is the oldest and strongest kind, said the horror fiction writer H. P. Lovecraft. Well 'fear' may be pitching it a bit strong in this context, but if you're anything like most people at this stage in the enquiry-answering process you're certainly feeling pretty nervous and possibly starting to panic. You've listened carefully to your enquirer. You've asked sensible questions. You know exactly what they want. Now your enquirer is waiting for you to help. And you haven't a clue where to start looking.

Fortunately, there are techniques for dealing with this. All you need is a little bit of thinking time. You can buy this time with a positive response – something like: 'I'm sure I can help; let me just think for a moment where would be the best place to start.' You'll pick your own form of words, of course, but having a response like this ready all the time is going to be really useful. First, it dispenses instant reassurance to the enquirer; you've promised to help. So, second, that means the enquirer will metaphorically step back and give you the few seconds' thinking time you need. Third, of course, a response like this commits you to nothing. It certainly doesn't commit you to finding the answer, because you don't know whether you can do that yet. But it does commit you to helping – and you can always help.

How? By exercising your imaginative thinking skills. Let's see how this works in practice . . .

Imagining the final answer

To deal with the 'fear' – or at least the panic – you need to turn the unknown into the known as quickly as possible: in this case, knowing where to go to find the information the enquirer needs. You've just bought yourself some thinking time to help you do this, so how are you going to make the best use of it? It's tempting to simply look busy – turn confidently to the nearest printed reference source you can find, or click onto a search engine and pretend you know what you're doing. Resist the temptation! You're wasting your time and the enquirer's with this pantomime, you're not getting yourself any nearer to a solution, and the enquirer will quite likely realize that you're just playing for time.

So you can actually do something much more useful with this thinking time: employ a fundamental technique of enquiry answering that you probably need to deploy with every enquiry you ever tackle. Remember we said in Chapter 1 that even if you rarely asked a hypothetical question of the enquirer, there was one hypothetical question that you almost always had to ask yourself? Well this is where it comes in – and the question is . . .

What is the final answer going to look like?

If you could magically see the answer in your mind's eye, on the page or on a screen, what would be in it and how would it be laid out? You can't yet see the fine detail – the actual words of the answer for instance – and you certainly don't know yet whether there is a source that will provide an answer that looks like that. But you do at least now know what you're aiming for and that will allow you to narrow down the options for where to look. Just as there was a posh phrase for the structured conversation we discussed in Chapter 1 – the reference interview – there's one for this process too: predictive search. Use the phrase if you like – but all it really means is starting to turn the unknown into the known, and that's a great way of helping you deal with the panic.

Just think of some of the forms the final answer could take . . .

Text is the lifeblood of any information and library service and it comes in many forms. It could be long, as in a book or report; short, as in an article or news item; or variable, as in a less formal document such as a single blog posting. In each of these cases, the text would be continuous, telling a coherent story from the beginning to the end of the document. But text can also be broken – designed to be read in little chunks – as in an encyclopaedia, dictionary, directory or series of blog comments. And it isn't necessarily printed; it can take the form of original manuscript records as well.

Tables of figures are scarcely less important. So much of human knowledge depends on counting and measuring that the answer you need will frequently include information presented numerically. This won't necessarily be static; the figures may be presented electronically, allowing them to be instantly updated whenever any of the data changes. And the practice of mashing data to produce new datasets just means that figures will continue to grow in importance.

Graphs or charts are just another way of presenting those figures that are so fundamental to human knowledge. They may lack the precision of the figures on which they're based, but they may be much more effective at demonstrating what the figures mean. They could be simply line or bar graphs, or pie charts, or even more visually rich infographics. (We'll come back to those in a moment.)

Lists are another bedrock of human knowledge and they come in many forms: checklists, directory entries, bibliographies, search results and new resources created by mashing lists together.

Images – whether still or moving – have grown hugely in importance for enquiry answering. Sharp pictures and video on the web have now replaced the muzzy photocopies from books and magazines that used to be all we could get. Like text, they come in many forms. With fine art, contemplation of the picture is sufficient in itself; illustrations usually support text; with news pictures or video, capturing the incident, vouching for its authenticity and publishing it quickly matters far more than technical quality; and then there are unimaginable quantities of self-published personal pictures and video clips.

Diagrams are just a stylized form of image designed to express something graphically. They can be technical, medical, managerial and much more. They may take the form of visually rich infographics – using graphs, charts, illustrations and summary text within a single design format to distil complex multifaceted topics in a brief and accessible form. They can be animated as well as static and, like the figures and the graphs, they can be updated in real time.

Maps are a further form of image and can illustrate just about anything.

Geo-spatial information is also fundamental to human knowledge, so we use maps to show topography, geology or climate, to illustrate trends, show economic, social or scientific information graphically, and to follow routes. They can be displayed diagrammatically, using conventional symbols, or can show a digitally enhanced version of the actual landscape, sometimes in three dimensions. No longer static and single-purpose, maps can now be both constantly updated and personalized.

Sound recordings can take the form of radio broadcasts, webinars, podcasts or momentary 'sound objects' like a sound effect or jingle. They can be delivered in a continuous stream in real time or packaged for replaying whenever required. Like images, sound now plays an infinitely more important part in answering enquiries as the web has developed.

You'll probably be able to think of many other forms the final answer could take now you've got the idea – but try not to think yet in terms of printed material, electronic documents or online content. That comes a bit later. Just think about what the final answer would look like, irrespective of the medium through which it's delivered.

While you're doing your thinking . . .

When you have the enquirer with you, they can see that you're going through a systematic procedure and they'll probably be happy to wait while you carry out your preliminary investigations. There's no great problem if you're using a text-based medium to deal with the enquiry either; you can sign off, do your thinking and get back to them as soon as you have something to report.

But using a voice-based medium, it's different. Silences can seem achingly long to the person at the other end, so it's a good idea to let the enquirer know what you're doing while you investigate – not necessarily a continuous running commentary but certainly a series of regular short bulletins explaining what you're finding and what you intend to do next. It may well be that the enquirer can also contribute ideas while this is going on, so it can in effect be a continuation of the structured conversation with which the process started. But be just slightly cautious if the enquirer starts suggesting actual sources to try at this stage; they may have some very good ideas of course – but remember that advising on possible solutions is your job, so don't risk being misled by a well-meant but ultimately ill-informed suggestion.

Of course you could put the enquirer on hold, leaving them to listen to an endless loop of music that isn't to their taste. But if you do that the enquirer has no idea what's going on – doesn't even necessarily know if you're still there – and their impatience may start to rise again. So if you think your preliminary investigations may take a little time, perhaps suggest that you'll call them back. Guarantee when you'll do that – and make sure you either meet or beat that deadline.

We'll have a look at how imagining what the final answer will look like – or predictive search if you will – works out in practice in a minute. But before we do that, there are some other important decisions you need to take as well: what are the best kinds of source and delivery medium to use, and do you have the resources to tackle the enquiry at all?

Choosing the best type of source and delivery medium

Make no mistake – the internet is a vital tool of enquiry work, and the web is the best single enquiry-answering tool we have. Screen-based media offer enormous advantages over print in allowing you to search rapidly through unimaginable quantities of content and providing instant access to your chosen information source. But the fact is that print on a page is still a uniquely valuable medium, and we should be very cautious about predicting its demise, because forecasts like that almost invariably come to grief.

Now these days that doesn't necessarily mean ink on paper. E-books are a widely accepted alternative and screen technology is improving all the time, making the content more and more comfortable to read and the experience increasingly close to that of reading ink on paper. Studies also suggest that reading content on a tablet computer may be a much pleasanter experience than on a laptop – although that's for you and your enquirer to judge at the time.

However, there's also evidence to suggest that people are increasingly finding e-books a less satisfactory experience than print on paper. Some studies show that people who read traditional print may actually retain more of what they read in memory, and may also need to read less of the document to understand its main themes than they might have to do if they were reading it on screen. Screen-based media still don't match the flexibility you can achieve by spreading opened books and magazines out on a desk, marking their pages, arranging them in piles. By all means browse online for information and ideas; but when it comes to serious reading, print – or at least a very good electronic substitute for it – is a far more comfortable medium to use.

So as well as deciding what the information your enquirer needs will look like, you also have to determine certain of its other characteristics. Only then can you decide on the kind of source that may be best suited to the purpose, and the best medium to use in delivering it. It's likely to be a crucial decision for the way you present the answer to your enquirer, and it's something you should have been able to determine from some of the Why? and How? questions you asked earlier. The characteristics of the subject that you need to consider at this stage are . . .

Focus, dynamism, complexity, viability

Focus: Is the information required broad-based and comprehensive or narrow and specific? For example: broad-based and comprehensive: 'cats'; narrow and specific 'British Birmans'.

We've already seen the dangers that can arise when an enquirer says 'Get me everything you've got on . . .'. It's very unlikely that they literally mean 'everything'. But sometimes people really do want a broad overview of a subject. They might be gathering background information as a preliminary to a more detailed study, or they may just want to brief themselves for a meeting, interview or short-term project. So here are some suggestions for types of source you could try. Don't worry too much about the delivery medium just yet – print or e-book, web page or PDF document – we'll come onto that later. Some of the ideas here may suggest print on paper to you – but try not to make that assumption yet.

For broad-based, comprehensive information, you could use:

- an entry in a general encyclopaedia
- a chapter in a textbook
- a complete textbook.

But if your enquirer has got beyond that stage, and is delving into a subject for more narrow and specific detail, you could try:

- an entry in a special encyclopaedia
- an index entry in a textbook
- a report from a specialist organization (i.e. not a conventional publisher)
- a journal article or news item
- a statistical table

- an entry in a directory
- a database record
- a website or page.

Dynamism: Is the information required static or dynamic? Static information is complete – finished. It's a matter of history. That's not to say that new research won't be done into it in the future but, to qualify as static, the subject must have reached a full stop at the time your enquirer asks you about it. Deciding whether information is static is a hazardous undertaking. Stonehenge may be thousands of years old, but if the enquirer is looking for information on new archaeological finds that tell us more about its purpose or method of construction, that means that the information required may not be static at all. Your When? or What? questions (trying to find out what aspect of Stonehenge the enquirer is interested in) should have helped you to establish that.

But, assuming that you are certain that the information you are being asked about really *is* static, print on the page (whether ink on paper or a high-quality e-reader) is going to be a perfectly acceptable way of satisfying it, and may offer a more comfortable reading experience than looking at, say, web pages with all their extraneous and off-putting surrounding content.

Dynamic information is changing now; a developing news story is a classic example of dynamic information. So you need to be sure that you've opted for a delivery medium that allows the enquirer to keep up with events. Nevertheless, there are degrees of dynamism; a weekly source – whether a printed journal or its online equivalent – may well be sufficient for keeping up to date with medical research, where the papers tend to be submitted months before publication. Stock market prices, on the other hand, can change second by second and require at least a near to real-time service to keep up with them.

So bearing in mind these variations in dynamism, you'll need to opt for a medium that will enable your enquirer to keep up with events as they happen. That's likely to mean a continuously or regularly updated medium such as a web page, or a feed (tracking updates to information on a particular site). These may not represent as comfortable a read as a printed book or e-reader page, but the need for the information to be as up to date as possible trumps the need for reading comfort.

One thing you may well find yourself having to do with dynamic information is browsing and scanning through the content you find. Because the information is changing fast, it may only have been indexed automatically, with no allowance for any of the synonymous, broader or narrower terms that you or the enquirer may have used (although growing use of semantic technology, taking account of the meaning of the words and the context in which they appear, will increasingly render this less of a problem). So you might have no alternative but to read quickly through quite a lot of text – a selection of news stories, perhaps, or a lengthy article. We'll look at strategic reading techniques to help you do this in Chapters 4 and 7.

Complexity: Is the information about a single concept, or is it multifaceted – concerned with how two or more concepts relate to one another?

Single-concept enquiries can almost always be summed up in a word or a short phrase – 'dogs' or 'town planning'. That doesn't necessarily mean, however, that information on them is going to be easy to find; you might be looking for rare occurrences of a single word or phrase buried in a mass of text. Nevertheless, to answer single-concept enquiries you might be able to find a book or an article (whether ink on paper, print in an e-book, a PDF document or a single website) using nothing more complex than your own library catalogue or discovery system or an all-purpose search engine.

Multifaceted enquiries, on the other hand, are concerned with the impact of one concept upon another – something like 'the health risks of rabies spreading from wolves in central Europe to domestic dogs' or 'the town planning law implications of non-retail uses of former shops in conservation areas'. To find acceptable answers to questions such as these you'll need to make more sophisticated use of search engines – using the power search option or Boolean logic, for example (more on these in Chapter 4). But you'll do even better if you identify a specialist database to search in the first place – a public health database in the first instance, perhaps, or an environmental one in the second. (We'll consider how to identify specific sources shortly.)

Finally, a word of warning: the focus, dynamism and complexity of any subject can all vary according to your perception of it. We've already seen that an enquiry's dynamism can be measured in minutes or years – and your perception of an enquiry's focus and complexity may well depend on the environment in which you work. If you work in an academic library that supports courses in statistics or demographics, then you'll probably regard the Welsh migration query as pretty general and none too complex either, whereas someone in an all-purpose reference library, or working for a specialist organization that normally has no need for demographic information at all, might see it as very specific and complex indeed. This leads us on neatly to . . .

Viability: Do you have the resources to answer this enquiry in-house, and if not is the answer likely to be found in a published source at all?

The first of these two problems is likely to be the easier to deal with. If you provide an information service that specializes in science, you probably won't have much in-house on the arts. You have access to all the resources of the free web of course – but so does your enquirer, so they're looking to you for more than that. They may expect you to be able to source documents on unfamiliar topics for them, or at the very least to advise on specialist institutions or sources that they could access or visit. A library in a law firm may be primarily concerned with law – but the litigation in which the firm is currently engaged may be concerned with any subject, and the lawyer will be expecting you to provide them with the background information they need to fight the case. Bear in mind, too, that there may be more information buried in your collections than you might ever have imagined; your library management system – if you use one – may be able to help you unearth it. (We'll come back to this in Chapter 8 on Choosing Your Toolkit.)

When it comes to whether the information your enquirer needs is in a published source at all, you're on much shakier ground. It's actually very difficult to say with any certainty that information isn't published anywhere. Even the most comprehensive of search engines, for example, still covers only a fraction of the content on the web – not to mention all the older documents that haven't been digitized yet and information from the many developing nations that still aren't well represented in mainstream resource guides or retrieval tools. And you can also be sure that, as soon as you tell your enquirer that the information they need isn't published, they'll find it themselves by serendipity. So this might be an occasion when you need to seek out not documents but expert help. But who to ask? We'll return to what to do when you can't find the answer in Chapter 5.

Print, electronic documents, online

The whole point about taking time to determine a subject's focus, dynamism and complexity is to help you decide which delivery medium would be most appropriate for the job. So before we try this out on some real enquiries, let's review the advantages and disadvantages of each.

Printed sources are easy to handle, user-friendly, carry no running costs and don't need electricity to make them work. You don't usually need to explain to an enquirer how to use a printed source, and print on paper is a very comfortable way of taking in information – so you can hand a printed source over with the minimum of initial help. But printed sources can also be out of date, slow to use if you are hunting for information buried in the text, and inflexible if their indexing doesn't accommodate the approach the enquirer wants to take. So they're only really good for static information.

Electronic documents means fixed content stored in a digital format. It could be a PDF document accessed online, an e-book read on a special reader, a journal delivered to a tablet computer, or (less likely these days) a publication or database on a CD-ROM. As with the printed sources, the content that electronic documents contain is fixed – once the document is published, that's it until the next edition. (And they have the further disadvantage compared with printed sources that they need electricity before you can use them.) However, unlike printed sources, they may enable you to search for information buried in the text reasonably quickly – albeit with varying degrees of sophistication (more on this in Chapter 4). So they can be quite good for finding more focused information.

Online services (delivered via a browser or an application on a tablet computer or smartphone) can be bang up to date, and the range of opportunities they offer for finding the one piece of information you need quickly are legion. But you do have to satisfy yourself that you can trust what you find, and you can be swamped with poor-quality information in the process. Often you'll need to take a decision on whether to go for a professionally edited specialist online service instead of just relying on the free web. If you do, you may find greater accuracy and searching flexibility – but you either have to pay for all the content you download or else need to ensure that the terms of your licence allow you to provide the information to your enquirer. But with these caveats, online services should be good for information that is dynamic and multifaceted.

Does all this really work?

Let's see how all this would work with just some of the questions that our different types of enquirer posed in Chapter 1. We'll start with a particularly straightforward one, to illustrate how the principle works and show just how precisely you can define the final answer using this technique. It's the one that started with a request for books on retailing.

What is Marks & Spencer's current pre-tax profit?

What will the final answer look like?	This is about as straightforward an answer to visualize as there can be – it's going to take the form of a single monetary figure, attached to a company name which you already know, with a very recent date.
Focus	Narrow and specific; the enquirer wants just one figure.
Dynamism	Could be very dynamic; the announcement might only have come this morning, or the last quarterly result might have been a couple of months ago – which begs the question: when is the next one due?
Complexity	Single concept; there's been no mention of the figure being put alongside other results – for example to produce accounting ratios – which could have turned it into a multifaceted enquiry.
Viability	It's a very common request, so it should be available in plenty of published sources, several of which will be accessible anywhere.
Likely type of source and delivery medium	The figure will certainly appear somewhere on paper, but because this is a business topic and timeliness is important, you're more likely to find it on a screen. All but the smallest of companies these days have a corporate website, so that's the obvious first place to look. Larger companies, like Marks & Spencer, also publish glossy annual reports, so that's an alternative. Failing that, you could try something that gives information on a lot of companies – such as a company directory or database. You could perhaps try the business pages of a newspaper to look for news of the company's latest results – but since you'd be looking for one specific piece of information buried among thousands of others, it would be far more sensible to use a searchable news website. But of all these possibilities, one source trumps all the rest: the company's own website. It's easy to find, will be guaranteed to have the most up-to-date figure, and – because company announcements are regulated by legislation and, in this case, by stock exchange rules too – you can trust the answer.

Get the idea? Now let's look at a few of the more complex enquiries.

I'm looking for information on migration patterns in Wales.

What will the final answer look like?	This is a request for information that will track and measure the movements of people. If it's about measurement then it will have to take the form of figures presented as statistics. However, there could be textual commentary on the figures, and they could also be presented as a graph, chart, infographic or diagrammatic map.
Focus	Depends what sources you have access to; it's pretty broad-based if you have plenty of statistical and demographic sources to hand and can offer the enquirer lots of options, but it's narrow and specific if you don't, because the enquirer wants one type of population data only.
Dynamism	Relatively static at the moment; censuses tend to be taken only at widely spaced intervals, albeit with more frequent intermediate population estimates. However, this is likely to change as more and more countries move on to rolling census-taking.
Complexity	Fairly multifaceted; although this is a standard census enquiry, it does involve combinations and permutations of figures about people and places.

Viability	Since plenty of government information is now published online, finding the basic data should present few problems. After that, though, it will depend on whether that data is available in a form that is useful to the enquirer, and how much additional information – such as commentary on the figures – they want.
Likely type of source and delivery medium	You're looking for statistics on the movement of people. Such comprehensive data could only be gathered by some sort of government agency, like a national statistical office. Because more and more government data is available online, you're likely to find much of it on the web, although more detailed analysis may be available in statistical serials published in electronic and perhaps printed form.
	But censuses aren't necessarily taken that frequently, so the latest available data could be a few years old; is there any way of updating it with interim estimates?
	Also, the enquirer may want to be able to manipulate the figures to mash the data into new datasets – in which case they're going to need it in a manipulable form, such as a spreadsheet.
	Finally, if the enquirer also wants commentary on these migration patterns, or maps and diagrams, they might be worth looking for in sociology or demographic textbooks – or possibly in a journal produced by the census-taking authority.

I'm doing a project on the Westminster Aquarium.

What will the final answer look like?	We're looking for information on a Victorian building in London – not a first-rank one either, like the Crystal Palace (which our muddled enquirer mentioned). There'll be descriptive text and pictures but, because it's not a particularly important building, you're probably not going to find very much about it in any one place.
Focus	Narrow and specific in that you're looking for information on just one building – but that may have to change if the enquiry turns out not to be viable.
Dynamism	Static; initial exploratory searching will reveal that this Victorian building was pulled down years ago, and was never of the first rank anyway. So pretty much anything you find, no matter how old, will probably be useful.
Complexity	Single concept; with an obscure topic like this, you can't afford to be choosy.
Viability	Hard to say. There will surely be some basic information available on the web, if only because virtually any topic, no matter how obscure, attracts its own enthusiasts. Whether you can find enough material on that narrow and specific topic to satisfy the requirements of the enquirer's assignment remains to be seen.
Likely type of source and delivery medium	Detailed textbooks on Victorian architecture or specialist guides to London's historic buildings may yield something, but because it's a relatively obscure building you're probably going to have to hunt through quite a lot of printed indexes to find anything at all. Perhaps the enquirer's idea of the *Illustrated London News* is worth following up – if the printed version has a decent index or if the archive has been digitized. As we've already surmised under the Viability heading, the building might even have 'friends' – enthusiasts who might share information about it on the web – but if you followed this up you'd need to be sure that the information they provided was reliable.

I need: local newspaper reports about council questions on immigrants; information on the Strong & Moral Britain Association – especially its funding; details of the obligations on school governors to declare other interests. And I don't want to use any online sources.

What will the final answer look like?	Quite a shopping list of different kinds of information here. For the reports on **council questions**, the enquirer suggested that only the printed local newspaper will do. You may end up having to go along with this, but a much better alternative would be the official record of council proceedings – provided it's still available in printed form. For the **association**, you need not only neutral directory-type information about its activities but also (because it's dubious) something probing and investigative, which probably suggests a searchable news or article source again – difficult because of the enquirer's ban on use of online services. The **school governor** information is going to take the form of rules, regulations, codes of practice – that sort of thing. These may well come in the form of a handy booklet published by the school, local education authority or central government education department. They could also take the form of legislation or official regulations.
Focus	Three quite narrow and specific enquiries, all linked in the enquirer's story.
Dynamism	Depends on which aspect you're investigating. The **council questions** on immigration could have flared up recently or might have been dormant for years. Ditto the stuff about the **association**; you'll certainly want the most up-to-date information you can get about its whereabouts, activities, governance and funding but don't know yet whether the neo-fascist issue is current or long past. And it will be important to have the current version of the **school governor** rules, but we don't know at the moment how frequently they change.
Complexity	Multifaceted throughout. The 'immigration questions' concept will need to be linked to the name of the councillor brother, and subsequently to the 'Strong & Moral Britain Association' and 'neo-fascism' concepts. But that's going to be really tricky if the enquirer continues to insist on not using online sources. It's going to involve a lot of manual searching and cross-referencing on paper. The rules for school governors are likely to be more straightforward because they'll be packaged somewhere – in a handbook or regulation. But it would still be helpful to home in quickly on the specific issue of declarations of interest. So this part is multifaceted too – albeit requiring the use of strategic reading rather than searching techniques, again because of the enquirer's ban on use of online sources.
Viability	Frustratingly, information on the council immigration questions and the Strong & Moral Britain Association are probably readily available on the web. But the enquirer won't allow that, so you're going to need to think imaginatively about alternatives. You may need to question the enquirer further about the likely timing of the council questions. Then coach them on how to scan quickly and effectively, whether using the local newspaper or the official council record (more on this in Chapter 4). And, finally, think laterally about how you might investigate the Strong & Moral Britain Association without using the most obviously viable tool – the web (again see Chapter 5 for ideas). So this part of the enquiry could be much less viable than might at first appear.

	The school governor rules should present fewer viability problems. Lots of people are school governors, they'll all need the rules and guidelines, so these are likely to be pretty accessible. But again you'll need to think laterally about how to access them not using the web.
Likely type of source and delivery medium	Delivery medium first of all: frustrating as it may be, print seems to be the only one you're going to be allowed to use. So what possible sources does that leave you with . . . ?
	As we've already established, the official record would be the most authoritative place to go for the **council questions** (so long as they're still published in print form – or even possibly on microfiche). Failing that, you may have to fall back on the local newspaper as the enquirer suggests – again perhaps dealing with microfiche as you go further back. The information you need is going to be thinly scattered through the various back issues, but at least their layout facilitates strategic reading.
	Basic information on the **association** might come from a printed directory of associations (see the Starter Sources in Chapter 8 for possible places to look). But that's unlikely to provide information on its more dubious activities. So maybe you're going to have to find a specialist to help you with this (more on that in Chapter 5). Fortunately you do at least have a precise name (assuming that the enquirer has got it right).
	Finding the rules for **school governors** would probably be so easy on the web that, again, it's deeply frustrating that you're not allowed to use it. It may be worth your while trying to negotiate a compromise answer with the enquirer on this. Since this is arguably the least contentious aspect of the subject, maybe they could be persuaded to allow you to use the web just for this item. (We'll look at compromise answers in more detail in Chapter 5.)

Identifying actual sources

So now at last we've reached the really hard part – trying to discover whether any actual sources exist that provide your ideal solution. This is the really daunting bit (isn't it?) – having to learn hundreds of sources and have their details always at your fingertips, so that you can be ready at all times to come out with an instant diagnosis that always seems so impressive when doctors do it. It's true – there are an awful lot of information sources available, and you can spend an entire career answering enquiries and still be discovering new sources on your very last day at work.

But reassurance is at hand. First of all, successful enquiry work depends on constant practice, so the more you do it, the easier it becomes because you can remember more sources without ever having consciously learned them. (Actually this can be a danger as much as an advantage; if you get too used to going to one particular source, you tend to continue using it even if a newer, more efficient one becomes available.) Second, if your service uses an integrated library management system, its discovery features will probably enable you to source information contained not just within your own collections but from wider resources outside as well. (We'll list some of these systems in Chapter 8 on Choosing Your Toolkit.)

But the really big reassurance is that you can function perfectly effectively by keeping just a few multipurpose reference sources in mind. Again, take a look at the list of Starter Sources in Chapter 8. Between them, they will get you started on a very high proportion of the enquiries you will encounter. As the title of the list implies, they are only a start, and many information professionals would no doubt dispute some of my choices and want to substitute alternative candidates of their own. Nevertheless, what these sources (or others like them) can do is set you on the track of other, more specialized sources that you can't possibly be expected to remember.

Learning some really useful ones

So the basic principle is: to get to know a limited number of the most useful sources that you have immediately to hand – whether physically in the library or available virtually through the discovery tools – plus a selection of really useful web-based resources that you know you can rely on. There's no great mystery to this. If you're working in a public reference or college library, it will already be well stocked with sources of this kind, and you can spend some time profitably in the early stages of your new job browsing through some of them to see what they can do for you.

Two tips. First, if you're operating from a traditional enquiry desk, concentrate first on the ones that are shelved immediately behind you. They will be the ones that your more experienced colleagues have found the most useful over the years. And second, when you are examining and evaluating an unfamiliar source, don't just flick or scroll through it at random, but make it do something for you. If it's a directory or a statistical journal, look up a specific organization or figure. If it's a printed source, follow up all the index references to a subject of your choice. If it's electronic, give it a really complex task to perform and see how quickly it responds and how relevant its answers are.

It would also be worth exploring any kind of know-how file that your colleagues may have compiled. It's likely to represent the fruit of years of accumulated collective experience of enquiry answering and (if you'll forgive the mixed metaphor) can be a goldmine of hard-to-find information, once tracked down never forgotten. It could take the form of a database on your intranet, a set of bookmarked favourite websites accessible centrally somewhere, a Frequently Asked Questions (FAQs) kind of offering or a wiki-type application to which colleagues can add whenever something strikes them as useful. Whatever form it takes, it will be well worth getting to know in detail, because it will be uniquely tailored to your own organization's information specialities and the kinds of questions your enquirers are in the habit of asking. (We'll return to resources of this kind in Chapter 6 when we look at signing off the enquiry.)

But what if you're operating on your own, with sole responsibility for the library or information service of a specialist organization and no one to turn to for help? Well, you could try going through the list of Starter Sources given in Chapter 8, visiting each of their websites in turn, where there is one, and seeing whether any of the featured sources might be of use to you. Many of them are professionally edited charged-for services, so the links will just take you to a description of the source from which you can make your judgement as to its value to you. But some of the Starter Sources are free, so you can obviously use those straight away.

And if you want to see any of the resources that are available in printed form, you could try awarding yourself an afternoon off, going to your nearest large public reference library or to your university, armed with the Starter Sources list, and ask to see as many of them as you can. Then use them to find out which journals, directories, statistical serials, websites and databases might help you in your work.

Coming next – smarter searching

Now that we have a pretty good idea which sources we're going to use, and the most efficient delivery media for the purpose, we can actually get down to looking things up. This can present plenty of pitfalls, which we as professionals need to learn to anticipate and avoid. So in Chapter 4, we'll think about strategies for efficient searching, and learn how to hone our systematic thinking skills.

To recap . . .

- **Remember that there are techniques you can learn for stopping your mind from going blank – without having to know any actual sources.**

- Begin by visualizing the final answer in your mind's eye – so you know exactly what you're looking for.
- Decide on the focus, dynamism, complexity and viability of the enquiry – it will help you determine the best kinds of sources and delivery media for the job.
- Only then start looking for specific sources, bearing in mind that a small number of multipurpose reference sources can get you started on a lot of enquiries.
- Above all, think imaginatively.

CHAPTER 4

Smarter searching

Developing efficient search strategies by thinking systematically

In this chapter you'll find out how to:

- **avoid traps for the unwary**
- **make the most of indexes and searching tools**
- **read strategically**
- **decide whether you can rely on what you find**
- **above all, think systematically.**

There's a saying in show business that amateurs rehearse so that everything goes right and professionals rehearse so that nothing goes wrong. It's a great definition of the difference between an amateur and a professional, in any profession.

Just think how it works with a show. Amateurs haven't a clue what could go wrong, so they have to rehearse everything equally. Professionals have the training, the knowledge, the experience to know where the danger points are in a production – the rapid scene change, the complex piece of business – and concentrate on those. Yet amateurs can manage to put on a good show eventually, with practice. And exactly the same applies to one of the most hazardous parts of enquiry work: searching.

The problem is that, since everyone has access now to an apparently limitless pool of instantly available information, anyone can assume that they're an expert searcher. So information professionals – the ones who earn their living by searching, or advising people on how to search – have to be able to demonstrate that there are ways of searching smarter, even when they're using exactly the same tools as their enquirers. What can distinguish you, the professional, from your enquirer, the amateur? A lot of it is down to thinking systematically.

Who needs to be able to search smarter?

The short answer is: everyone. It doesn't matter whether you're doing the searching yourself or helping others to do so, you need to understand the principles behind it so that the whole process happens as smoothly and efficiently as possible. Just think why . . .

If you're working in a **public reference library** you may well find yourself dealing with people to whom searching doesn't come naturally. A personal visitor may require a lot of hand-holding while you help them discover the information they need. At the same time, a queue may be building up at the enquiry desk – or, if you've gone on an expedition to the shelves with your enquirer, other people may start hovering round waiting for you to become free. So however you decide to help, you have to make sure that your search strategy will work, quickly. If the enquiry has come in by phone, and you've agreed to do some preliminary searching on the enquirer's behalf – seeking out some likely references, for example – then you'll have agreed a deadline with them and you'll need to be sure that you can meet it, even if you encounter complications along the way.

It may be a bit different in a **school, college or university library**. Of course, you're not going to research the student's assignment for them; that's their job. But you have a vital role nevertheless in ensuring that they learn good searching habits from the outset – not bad ones. So you're likely to be suggesting search strategies they can adopt when they come to you seeking help. And when their search doesn't work for any reason, it's you they'll be turning to for advice on why it hasn't and what they can do to remedy the situation. And if they contact you for advice in advance of a visit, you may find yourself at the very least having to do trial searches yourself before you can help them. Information literacy – knowing how to find information and whether you can trust it when you do – is a fundamental life skill now, and it is part of your job to nurture that skill in students.

If you're a researcher in a **specialist organization** then you may well be responsible for the entire process – from taking the initial enquiry to delivering the finished answer, with a hefty amount of desk research to do along the way (more on all this in Chapter 7 by the way). Obviously in these circumstances, your smarter searching skills are paramount. Your enquirer probably won't be interested in how you arrived at the answer, but they will want to be satisfied that the answer you've provided is accurate, complete and reliable. Remember, too, that your enquirer may actually be pursuing their own (perhaps less efficient) researches in parallel to yours. It can be very embarrassing if they turn up serendipitously something that you've failed to find when supposedly searching systematically.

Just as in any other profession, there's a wealth of specialized technical and theoretical learning behind searching, which grows more and more multilayered the more sophisticated the available tools become. At its most advanced, this now means Big Data: highly skilled data analysts developing complex tools to extract useful information buried deep within unimaginable quantities of unstructured content. But at the day-to-day human level, the fundamental principles of smarter searching needn't be rocket science; at its most basic, it's a question of anticipating where the pitfalls lie and making sure they don't happen. A lot of that simply comes with practice – and particularly from getting into the habit of thinking systematically. So some tips on smarter searching . . .

Working out your search strategy

Because we began by imagining what the final answer would look like, and worked out the likely delivery media by determining the enquiry's focus, dynamism and complexity, we already have a list of potential sources that we could try. So it's obviously wisest to go to the one that's likely to give the best results first. Why? Because if we do find the answer there we can stop looking, secure in the knowledge that the other sources on our list would have been less fit for purpose. And what do we mean by 'fit for purpose'? That means deciding whether we need . . .

- the most **up-to-date** source (bearing in mind that up-to-dateness can vary from years to seconds)
- the one most **relevant** to the subject
- the one most **appropriate** for the task in hand.

Let's see how this might work with some of the enquiries we've been dealing with.

I'm looking for information on migration patterns in Wales.
Numerical census data is the core to all this. It wins on two of the three counts: it's **relevant** (all about population and their movements) and **appropriate** (you're looking for figures, at least to begin with). It may also be as **up to date** as you're going to get, even though full censuses tend to be taken at fairly

infrequent intervals. However, you may also have to consider where to look for later estimates of population movements since the last census; they should be more **up to date** but will probably be less detailed. And since the enquirer is trying to identify migration patterns, then informed commentary on the trends – in textbooks or journal articles – would also be both **relevant** and **appropriate** to the approach the enquirer wants to take.

I'm trying to find a song called When I Would Sing Under the Ocean [but the title is probably wrong].
Go for the most **relevant** source first – an encyclopaedia or dictionary (whether print or electronic) or reliable website that lists song titles – or perhaps an app that can recognize musical themes. It doesn't necessarily have to be particularly **up to date**, since you've already established that it's a more traditional song, not one that's likely to be currently in the charts – unless your enquirer wants to buy a recording, in which case some kind of **up-to-date** resource (such as an online record store) will be essential. Of course, all the evidence so far suggests that the title is wrong and that no amount of looking up, in print or electronic sources, is going to unearth it. So it may turn out that asking a musical expert is the most **appropriate** course of action.

Do you have the Electoral Register [because I'm trying to trace people with a particular surname]?
The Electoral Register (the local one we presume) may technically be the most **relevant** source because that's what the enquirer asked for. But, as we've already established when questioning them about what they were looking for, using the Register wouldn't be a particularly efficient way of finding people with a particular surname. Also, although it's updated every year, its entries can still go out of date pretty quickly – so it may not even be the most **up-to-date** source to try either. As we discussed with the enquirer, more **appropriate** sources might include genealogical sites, or specialist sites that track concentrations of surnames, or possibly social networking services that profile individuals – so these would probably represent the best starting point.

Searching systematically

Now you've decided how you're going to set about your searching, what are you going to search for? Plenty of things can go wrong – things that we as professionals ought to be able to avoid – so among the myriad things that can cause problems, here are some that you should certainly consider:

Variant spellings

It doesn't matter whether you're using a printed index or a search engine, variant spellings can cause big problems. So try to anticipate them. Proper names are especially tricky; it was Cain who killed Abel in the Bible story, but Citizen Kane who had a sledge called Rosebud in the eponymous movie. And where on earth do you start looking for the fast food chain that calls itself *McDonalds* but dubs its culinary pièce de résistance a Big *Mac*? Also, many of the best reference resources – whether print or electronic – are American, so you may have to watch out for 'color' instead of 'colour', 'disk' instead of 'disc', 'skeptical' instead of 'sceptical'.

This may not be a great problem with printed indexes; your eye will quickly spot the difference. Large-scale search engines, too, may well help you by automatically attempting to fill in the rest of your search statement before you've even finished typing it. But you can't necessarily rely on this feature being available on simpler search engines embedded within individual websites – so if you search for 'favourite' or 'labour' on an American website it may keep on giving you a zero result no matter how much you swear at it. There are plenty of other pitfalls with variant spellings in British English too – jails can be gaols, choirs can be quires (in more archaic sources anyway) – one could go on but that's enough.

Homonyms

These are words with the same spelling that have more than one meaning. If you're looking for do-it-yourself supplies and keep coming up with foodstuffs instead, you've hit the homonym problem associated with 'nuts', which is equally at home in the two phrases 'nuts and bolts' and 'monkey nuts'. Scholars studying the indented wax symbols at the base of legal documents run the risk that their hunt for 'seals' will lead them to sea mammals. You need to be particularly alive to the dangers of homonyms, and be ready with tactics for taking evasive action if necessary. It's particularly – but not exclusively – a problem with free-text searching – i.e. when you're not able to take advantage of any controlled vocabulary feature such as an online taxonomy.

You can reduce the risks associated with homonyms by adding a further qualifying term to your search – such as 'food or 'crops' for 'nuts' and 'manuscripts' for 'seals'. But this technique can also raise further complications; if you try to qualify 'nuts' with a term like 'hardware', your qualifying term also has two definitions: do-it-yourself materials or computing equipment. So in this case, using a trade classification code (if it's possible to search on those in the source you're using) instead of the word will probably be a better option. In fact, whenever you're searching electronically, do keep an eye out for any links that look as if they might lead to an onboard thesaurus or other authority file of preferred terms that can help with your searching precision. And no matter how careful you are at anticipating the challenges presented by homonyms, you could still come to grief with a word like 'gross' – which can mean 'repellent', 'disgusting', 'fat', 'before the tax has been taken off' or '144'.

British versus American terminology

We've already seen some of the problems that American spellings can throw up, and of course it's exactly the same with American terminology – words that are different in British and American English. We all watch Hollywood movies (or do we mean films?), so most people would probably remember to use 'elevator' instead of 'lift', 'streetcar' or 'trolley' instead of 'tram', and 'pants' instead of 'trousers' (although this last one presents its own special homonym problems as well; 'pants' can also mean short, fast breaths, or be a slang term for 'useless' or 'bad'). But other differences may not spring to mind so quickly: a 'saloon' car in Britain is a 'sedan' in the USA; an American 'tap' (note the homonym problem here too) is a 'faucet'.

Finally, too, remember that dates are cited differently in America and Europe. As all the world knows following the tragic events at the World Trade Center, 9/11/2001 is 11 September in America – but in most of the rest of the world it's 9 November. So if you're using a search engine that permits date searching, make sure you have the elements in the right order.

Making the most of indexes

Really well constructed indexes are based on a thesaurus which allows for all the different approaches that a searcher could take towards a subject. Alas, however, the real world is full of ineptly constructed indexes. An 'amateur' index, maybe compiled by the book's author, might be full of elementary mistakes that a professional indexer would avoid. Such indexes might include an entry for 'railways', for example, but fail to add a parallel one or a reference for 'train services'. A professional indexer – a member of the Society of Indexers, for example – would avoid such mistakes; but a professional indexer will probably be on a fixed fee based on the estimated time taken to complete the job, so may not have the time to index down to the level of detail that would be helpful to you.

But, you might be thinking, why are we worrying about printed indexes at all when there are so many rapid electronic searching aids available? Well first, don't imagine that your experience is necessarily going to be any better if you're using a search engine; it's only going to be as good as the algorithm that drives it and the words and phrases that are available for it to index. (We'll come back to this in a minute.) And in any case, there's evidence that people are finding newer media such as e-books a less comfortable read than they might initially have expected – so it's far too early to write off print on paper yet, or the printed indexes that go with it. In fact, it's wise to assume that, whatever kind of index you encounter, whether presented as a printed alphabetical list or a searchable file using some kind of electronic retrieval tool, it will have its limitations and there will come a point where you will have to fend for yourself.

Synonymous, broader, narrower and related terms

When you were discussing the task with your enquirer, you or the enquirer are likely to have jotted down a list of possible words and phrases to search under. That's fine as far as it goes, but with only a little extra effort, you can create a far more valuable searching aid for yourself. So instead of just jotting down those words and phrases randomly, in the order they occur to you, try listing them in a structured way. Creating your own **mini-taxonomy** – specially designed to help you with your current enquiry – should enable you to . . .

- construct logical search strategies that link concepts to each other unambiguously
- try the most specific terms first and pull back systematically until you start finding useful information

- and ensure that, if you do have to go back to a source you've looked at already, you only need to look for new terms and don't risk repeating previous searches.

In other words, it's a pretty powerful searching tool – not just for you of course, but also for a student doing an assignment or a member of the public seeking to become self-sufficient with their searching. By introducing your enquirers to techniques such as these you'll be helping them improve their information literacy and empowering them as well.

Let's see how it might work in practice. Suppose you're researching – or helping someone to research – information on reptiles of the Galapagos Islands. As your enquirer has been explaining their needs in response to your questioning, you should have been jotting down possible search terms – words and phrases to search under. (If you've been left on your own to do the research on someone else's behalf, you can think of possible search terms by discussing the subject with a colleague and, again, noting down likely words and phrases as you talk together – or you can even discuss the subject with yourself if there's no one else to help.) Anyway, whatever you do, this is the list you've ended up with:

reptiles
Galapagos Islands
animals
islands
Pacific Ocean
tortoises
iguanas
volcanic terrain
fauna
equator

Not a bad start, but it takes only another minute to turn this into a far more valuable searching aid. What you need to do first is to separate these words and phrases according to the different concepts they represent. There are clearly two concepts here, the animals and the place, and – guess what? – we're back with the Who? What? When? Where? Why? How? that we used when originally discussing the enquirer's needs. So here are all those terms again, but rearranged this time according to the concepts they represent:

Who?	Where?
reptiles	Galapagos Islands
animals	islands
tortoises	Pacific Ocean
iguanas	volcanic terrain
fauna	equator

The last stage in the process of making all your terms fit for use in searching is to rearrange them one more time, into a natural hierarchy. This time, we'll just focus on the Who? concept. The enquiry is about 'reptiles', remember – so let's call 'reptiles' your **root term**. Then looking down the list again you can see a couple of **broader terms** – the generic word 'animals' and the more scientific one 'fauna'. Finally, you have some **narrower terms** – words that fit within the category of 'animals' or 'fauna' and also within the 'reptiles' category; these terms are 'tortoises' and 'iguanas'. So you'd end up with a mini-taxonomy that looked like this:

Broader terms	animals, fauna
Root term	reptiles
Narrower terms	tortoises, iguanas

Now if you're inclined to think that this is all a rather tedious process to have to go through, just bear three things in mind. First, this is a deliberately simple example to demonstrate the principles clearly; you'll frequently find yourself dealing with much more complex concepts than this, encompassing many more possible terms to juggle with. Second, if you're not doing the research yourself, but helping a student or a member of the public to do it, your use of this technique can both help them to work more efficiently – and hence finish the job quicker – and also demonstrate to them that you are a professional who knows where the pitfalls lie and how to avoid them. And third, we'll discover in a moment how this process really pays dividends when you start applying it to the indexes you use in your researches – again, whether you're dealing with a printed alphabetical index or terms retrieved by a search engine. So let's start to see just how useful it can be.

Printed indexes

It's when things start to go wrong that your careful preparation for searching will really pay off. Hunting for information is a journey into the unknown. Every source you use will be differently constructed, and have its own indexing quirks. As your searching progresses, you're bound to come across relevant words and phrases that you never thought of in the first place. If you do, your mini-taxonomy should at least help to ensure that you don't risk repeating work you've already done. Let's go back to those reptiles; suppose you've looked through a few printed sources, and you suddenly find the following entry:

iguanas *see* land iguanas, marine iguanas

A 'see' reference should mean that the indexer has decided to put no index entries under the term you used, and is redirecting you instead to (in this case) two different places where you should find all the relevant index entries for each kind of iguana. Alphabetically they're widely separated, so you'd never have found them in a printed index if the indexer hadn't given you this essential guidance. So the first thing you need to do is amend your mini-taxonomy like this:

Broader terms	animals, fauna
Root term	reptiles
Narrower terms	tortoises, iguanas
Subset of narrower term	land iguanas, marine iguanas

The second thing is decide whether or not to go back over previous sources and recheck them for the new terms. This is where your systematic approach again pays dividends, because if you do decide to go back to previous sources, you can do so secure in the knowledge that you only have to check under the newly discovered terms, since you can guarantee that you've already searched systematically under the terms you thought of in the first place. If there's nothing extra to be found under the new terms, then you should be able to abandon the source without wasting any more time on it. (We'll discuss efficient management of your time in Chapter 5.) Anyway, back to your printed index searching and the next thing you come across is:

reptiles *see also* predators

This is the indexer trying to be helpful. Since many reptiles are predators, they've judged that anyone looking for reptiles might either be interested in broadening their search out to include predators in general or, alternatively, may be interested only in the predatory habits of reptiles – not their habitats, mating rituals or whatever. With a '*see also*' reference, you should expect to find entries in both places in your printed index – the place where you originally looked and the additional place that you've been directed to – because the two terms are not the same and don't appear in the same place in the taxonomy that you've created. In this context, 'predator' is a **related term**. It doesn't fit in your mini-taxonomy at all, because – unlike reptiles such as snakes or crocodiles – tortoises and iguanas are exclusively herbivores. But it's far better to be alerted to the possibility of further terms to search under than not, and that's the function of '*see also*' references in printed indexes.

Electronic search tools

Electronic media can offer a whole range of additional searching aids, locating terms with a speed and accuracy that you usually can't match using a printed index. Such tools include search engines – whether a large-scale generic search engine or a search window on a specific website – the discovery tools within your library management system, and other more limited finding tools of the kind that you might encounter using a PDF reader, browser or e-book reader. We need to consider all these separately.

Search engines can, for example, save you the bother of thinking of all the forms in which your search term could appear by automatically looking for other words with the same root as the one you've used. If you're doing a search on surface transport, for instance, and put in the term 'rail', the search engine could come back with references to 'railway' and 'railroad' (but might also retrieve documents on 'railings', so you have to be constantly on your guard). If you've mistyped something, a search engine might well suggest a correct spelling. Increasingly, too, search engines will try to anticipate what you're looking for, coming up with possible words or phrases even before you've finished typing, and thereby perhaps alerting you to better terms to search on as a result.

Some so-called 'clustering' search engines will take the top hundred results and break them down by subject, giving the enquirer a good overview of the way the search engine is looking at the subject. Index or directory-based search engines, which work on a strict hierarchy of terms, can also provide extra ideas for terms to search on when you're putting your search strategy together. And yet other search engines can even accommodate natural-language searching, attempting to parse a complete sentence or phrase for its sense and returning an immediate, finished answer. So there are a myriad ways in which search engines can help you improve your search strategy and hence your chances of success.

But the problem is that – unlike a printed index, which you can potentially assess in its entirety – you can't easily determine the way a search engine does its indexing. Search engines crawl websites (or, in the case of an embedded search engine, one specific website) looking for terms to index, and then an algorithm interrogates the index, trying to match your search to the indexed terms. But this actually raises several important issues. First, it's not just one algorithm for all search engines but potentially hundreds, which means that each search engine does its job differently, giving sometimes widely varying results for the exact same search. Second, this whole process is invisible to you; you don't really know what the search engine has done. And third, an algorithm is only a formula, applying logic to the task but without any knowledge of the reason or motive for the interrogation.

There are further issues here that you won't normally encounter when using printed indexes. A search result might begin with automatically sponsored links, which benefit the search engine provider if you click on them but won't necessarily help you find what you want. Also, many website designers have now got search engine optimization down to a fine art, ensuring that their site comes to the top of the list in response to your search, even though it may not be the best place to go from your point of view.

Searching software will also probably attempt to return results ranked for relevance – but that simply means that the algorithm automatically tries to determine the importance of a document to your search according to things like how frequently your search term appears in it, whether it's in the title or on the home page, or how frequently the document is linked to from others. So choose the right search engine for the task in hand. If you know the keywords you want to search with, choose a free-text search engine. If you need a comprehensive set of results, try a metasearch engine. And if you're interested in content from social media, choose a search engine that focuses on content from that kind of medium.

Underlying all this is the fact that – contrary to widespread popular belief – *there is more than one search engine*. There are in fact hundreds and it's worth exploring some of them to see what special features they can offer in dealing with various different kinds of search you'll need to do. (See Chapter 8 on Choosing Your Toolkit for where to find listings of some of the main ones.) The key message that you as an information professional need to take away is this: a search engine might help to narrow the field of your search – but no matter how sophisticated its construction, no algorithm can replicate the rich complexity of thought going on in your head. As you search, you're assessing each document retrieved and constantly relating it in your mind to what the enquirer actually needs. No algorithm can do that. A search engine can frequently give you a good start, but that's probably all.

Library management systems will incorporate discovery tools that probably enable you to interrogate external resources as well as the collections you hold in-house. (Again, we've listed some of them in Chapter 8.) But the same limitation applies as with search engines; the results will only be as good as the algorithms that drive the searching software. They'll deliver a shortlist of possible sources for you to consider, but the final decision on which (if any) are likely to prove really useful to your enquirer is up to you.

Other electronic finding tools have even more limitations. A PDF reader will let you search for any word or phrase in the document you're reading, and can offer extra help by displaying the retrieved terms in the context in which they appear, so you can decide which might be the best occurrence of the term to look at first. It can also find different forms of a word – if you type in 'employ', it should also retrieve 'employs', 'employer's', 'employing', 'employment' and so on. But it will only find additions to the exact character string you enter, and can't suggest possible alternatives with different spellings. So if you enter 'employment' and the concept always appears in the document as the word 'job' or 'occupation', you won't find what you need even though the concept of employment may have been there all the time.

Similar considerations apply to the tool supplied with browsers that lets you find words or phrases buried in the web page you're looking at, and to the limited string searching facilities usually available on e-books. If for example you're searching for the word 'unction' (unlikely, I realize, but you never know!) tools like these are likely to additionally present you with the unhelpful result 'functionality'. Generally speaking, these relatively limited searching tools tend to force you to think of all the synonymous, broader, narrower and related terms for yourself – and that comes back to your mini-taxonomy.

Advanced search capabilities, which many search engines offer, can really help you exploit your mini-taxonomy to good effect. Whether you're using a large-scale generic search engine or one embedded within a single site, take a look around in the vicinity of the search window to see if there's a link to an advanced search or 'power' search option. To be honest, this may not always be easy to find; it may simply be an option behind a discreet little tools button that doesn't appear until after your first search results have come up. But, whichever search engine you're using, it's frequently worth persevering to try to find the advanced search option because it can help exponentially improve your search results.

Advanced search interfaces come in various different forms. They can be presented as a simple matrix that will allow you to be as flexible in your searching as you need. Or they may be more prescriptive, giving you pre-set options – for example retrieving only documents in which all of a given set of terms appear, or documents that contain any one or more of a selection of words, or specifying that you want to search for a specific phrase. Depending on the site, the advanced search feature can sometimes also allow you to limit your search by date and place (the When? and Where? concepts). Whatever form the advanced search interface takes, you're likely to be able to make good use of it if you're doing a complex, multifaceted search with many different terms to describe each concept.

Boolean logic is what drives advanced searching and it's really helpful for any searcher to be able to understand how this works in principle because it can be a very powerful retrieval tool indeed. It works by linking words or phrases together using the logical operators OR, AND and NOT. In fact, if you're adept at applying Boolean logic, you could try bypassing the advanced search option and using Boolean directly in the basic search engine window, typing in not only the search terms you want to use but also the logical operators provided by your chosen search engine that show how you want the terms to relate to one another. There may also be specialist symbols or commands that enable you to restrict the output to particular types of documents – PDFs for instance – and there may even be some limited provision for finding synonyms of your chosen search term. The symbols and syntax that you need to use for your Boolean searching vary from one search engine to another, but you can see how it works in principle on the next page.

A word of warning though: generic search engines may not cope well with sophisticated Boolean logic. They're designed on the assumption that they're predominantly being used by non-specialists, with the emphasis on simplicity of use rather than sophistication. However, if you're working with professional specialist databases – accessed through a commercial aggregator for example – as opposed to what you might pull up using a generic search engine, then you may well be able to construct searches based entirely on Boolean logic and using quite sophisticated syntax. Using professional

A search on ...	retrieves ...	and the result is ...
tortoises OR iguanas	all the documents on tortoises, all the documents on iguanas and (therefore) all the documents that mention them both together as well.	you get high **recall** (a lot of documents retrieved) but not necessarily high **relevance** because this search retrieves absolutely everything, including documents that contain only passing references to either species.
tortoises AND iguanas	only the documents that mention both tortoises and iguanas.	you get lower **recall** (because you retrieve none of the documents that mention only tortoises or only iguanas) but quite possibly higher **relevance** because the smaller number of documents retrieved might focus specifically on tortoises and iguanas together.
tortoises NOT iguanas	documents that mention tortoises, but not when they also mention iguanas.	you get somewhat lower **recall** (because you've excluded all the iguana documents), but you may have compromised your **relevance** too, because you've also excluded some potentially relevant tortoise documents – the ones that also mentioned iguanas.

databases, you could, for example, construct a search that says: 'I want all the documents on tortoises or iguanas of the Galapagos Islands, except for marine iguanas, which I want to exclude.' In straightforward Boolean logic (ignoring the specific symbols and syntax that any given professional searching software might use), that might look like this:

((tortoises OR iguanas) AND "galapagos islands") NOT marine

Searching efficiently, making the most of all the tools and techniques available, is a significant skill in its own right. So if you want to be really effective at it – and to be able to advise your enquirers authoritatively on searching techniques that they can deploy for themselves – it's worth reading up on the subject constantly and going on regular training courses to keep up to date with the latest innovations.

Reading strategically

Sometimes none of the searching tools at your disposal work. You may find yourself dealing with a printed document whose title and contents page suggest that it's going to be relevant, but it doesn't have an index in which you can look up the precise topic you're interested in. Or you may have retrieved a lengthy PDF document or densely packed web page, but the simple word-search tools provided can't confirm your suspicion that the document is likely to be useful because you're not using the same terminology as the author has chosen. In these circumstances, rather than ignoring a potentially useful source, you may have no option but to skim through the actual text, looking for the nuggets of relevant information that you're pretty sure must be in there. It may sound daunting, but there are ways of tackling this. The trick is knowing which words you can safely ignore.

Now we haven't lost sight here of the possibility that you might not be doing the searching yourself but supporting a student or member of the public in their researches. Hopefully, you've already demonstrated your professionalism in helping them avoid the searching traps that many amateurs might fall into. So now's your opportunity to empower your enquirer even more by introducing them to some basic strategic reading techniques. Here are the main ones that you can try:

Read down the **middle of the page**, relying on your peripheral vision to spot significant words. Try not to swivel your head; if you do that, persistence of vision will kick in and everything will blur. Alternatively, if you're faced with long lines of print, you can **bounce your eye** from the left half to the right half of the page, stopping and sampling the text each time. If you use this technique, do make sure that you stop momentarily each time to allow the characters to stop 'dancing' and give your eyes a chance to spot anything that might be significant.

So what are you looking for? Well, perhaps for **significant words and phrases** that will indicate you're on the right track. Once again, your trusty mini-taxonomy should tell you what those words and phrases are, including synonymous, broader, narrower and related ones. (Go back to an earlier point in this chapter to check up on this procedure.) However, the problem with this is that, if they're all in lower case, those words and phrases won't look any different to the eye from all the other text around them.

So instead, there's actually a really good win-win technique that you can apply. The characters that are most easy to spot, because they stand out from the rest of the text, also offer the best clues as to the document's content. So try loosening your focus a bit and looking, not for specific words, but for characters that are a different shape from the common herd – characters such as . . .

- **Capitalized words**: These are the names of people, organizations, places, possibly even concepts. They're the sorts of words that will indicate if you're on the right track.

- **Abbreviations:** These are shortened forms of the names of those organizations – or possibly concepts. So they offer similar clues to those provided by the capitalized words.
- **Numerals:** As we saw in Chapter 3, counting and measuring forms the basis of a great deal of human knowledge, so numerals of any kind – numbers, percentages, dates, monetary values – can also give you valuable clues as to the document's relevance to your enquiry. When you spot a numeral, pause, cast your eye to left and right seeing what's being measured, and decide whether it's relevant.
- **Words in non-standard typography:** Text in bold, italic or small capitals is also easy to spot and may offer valuable clues. Be slightly wary of these, though. Unlike with abbreviations and capitalized words, the decision to emphasize something using non-standard typography is a subjective one made by the author, so may reflect what the author believes is important, not necessarily what you're looking for.

And finally – a couple of first-rate techniques for getting through longer documents really quickly . . .

- **Read the first sentence of each paragraph:** If the paragraphs are reasonably long – say more than three sentences – it's astonishing how easy it is to follow a document's main argument by just reading the first sentence of each. Of course, this technique doesn't work when each paragraph is just a couple of sentences; you have to read so much of the document that you're unlikely to save yourself much time, so one of the other strategic reading techniques may be more appropriate. But when the paragraphs are longer, you can get through an enormous amount of text extraordinarily quickly using this technique – acquiring along the way such a clear idea of what the document is about that you might even begin to wonder why all the other sentences are there at all.
- **Spotting hidden signposts:** Besides helping you to get through lengthy documents at incredible speed (your students will love you forever if you introduce this technique to them), the first-sentence technique can also to help you to spot 'hidden' signposts – sentences and phrases that indicate the document's structure even though there are no actual headings or subheadings to break up the text. If you spot a first sentence that begins 'My next point is . . .', 'Moving on to . . . ' or 'And finally . . .', a document's structure can become as clear as if it was peppered with formal headings.

Reading at your normal reading speed

If you've ever done a speed-reading course, you'll recall that the techniques you were taught were probably designed to help you get through a document's complete text faster. But strategic reading techniques, like those shown above, don't do that. They work on the principle that you're reading at your normal reading speed, but being more selective about what you read, reasonably secure in the knowledge that you have picked the best bits of the document for your purposes.

However, a word of warning: none of these techniques is a panacea. Everything works some of the time, but nothing works every time. This is particularly true if you're trying to read documents on screen – web page, PDF, e-book. The screen flickers, the lights flicker, and the resolution is frequently better on the simplest of office printers. So it's worth considering printing out the Conclusions, Recommendations or Findings – or perhaps the Abstract or Executive Summary – and reading from the printed text of that instead. (There's a lot more about exploiting documents in this way in Chapter 7.)

Making sure that what you find is reliable

Years ago you used to be able to work on the principle that, if you saw a piece of information in three different places, it was probably true. Then along came the web – the ultimate vanity publishing medium. Now anyone can publish anything, regardless of whether or not they know what they're talking about, and an error on one website can be replicated over and over again on others. And not just errors either; in what's coming to be regarded as a 'post-truth' era, deliberate falsehoods – published with self-seeking or malign intent – can be accepted and spread by others either uncritically or because they accord with their own world view. This last is particularly important for people who rely exclusively on social media for their information. Social media algorithms tend to offer users more of the same, based on their previous online activity – thus risking depriving them of the opportunity to broaden their awareness or encounter any views contrary to their own.

So before we leave the issue of smarter searching, we need to think about whether you can believe what you find. Once again, this is a crucial lesson to get home if you're helping someone else with their researches too. Part of information literacy is being able to evaluate what you find – and if you're supporting students, for example, an essential part of your role as a responsible information professional is to encourage the habit of evaluation whenever you can. So what practical steps can you take?

Quality-controlled sources

First, start by using professionally edited, quality-controlled sources if you possibly can. Rather than just using a search engine straight away, begin by looking up likely sources for the information you need in a directory, bibliography or source guide – the kinds of resources you can see in the list of Starter Sources in Chapter 8. Sources like these have some measure of editorial control exercised over them, so they're much safer to use than just calling up a search screen on the web and hoping for the best. Obviously, they don't necessarily restrict themselves to resources on the free web; they may well include references to authoritative printed and electronic documents, and to charged-for services delivered online. But probably the commonest type of information they provide is web links, so, using such sources, you can get to useful places on the web just as quickly as you might when using a search engine – but with far more confidence that you can trust what you find.

And when you do start exploring likely places on the web, try following links from the sites that the quality-controlled sources recommended to other relevant sites. If you've satisfied yourself that the site you initially use is reliable, then the sites that it links to are pretty certain to be reliable as well. So this is an altogether safer way of exploring resources on the web than simply going back to a set of search engine results and trying the next one on the list in the hope that it will be better. Beware, though: the web is full of tempting byways. So make sure you keep track of where you've visited, and also that you're still really addressing the enquirer's needs. It's all too easy to get sidetracked.

Who's saying it and what's their agenda?

Once you think you're on to something that might provide the answer, you need to screen it for two things: authoritativeness and agenda. If you're using a printed source or an electronic document, look round the preliminary material – introduction, preface, blurb, 'about the author' – to determine how qualified the author is to merit your trust. If you've reached a potentially useful website, consider its top level domain (or TLD). If it's a .gov (government or public agency) or a .ac (academic institution), does that make the site inherently more trustworthy? Well, it might – but bear in mind that, while some .gov sites may be authoritative and expert, others may be more overtly political. And that the quality and reputation of academic bodies can vary from one institution, and one country, to another.

If you're dealing with a .com, .co or .org site, you could perhaps see what you can deduce about its standing by looking at its 'About us' page. If, for example, you read that alternative energy is inherently more cost-effective long term than nuclear power, you need to know whether it's being said by a research team (which may or may not be funded by industry), an energy supplier, energy industry organization or environmental pressure group. If you're doing the research on somebody else's behalf, providing information on the authoritativeness and agenda of the source you've used isn't an optional extra, it's an essential part of the answer. If you're supporting a student in their researches, then inculcating in them the habit of always determining a source's authority and agenda is one of the best services you can render. (There's quite a bit more on quality indicators in Chapter 6.)

Trust no one!

So is there any kind of source that you can trust implicitly? Probably not. Even the most reliable reference sources go out of date, so at the very least you need to decide whether what you're using matches the dynamism of the enquiry. Printed sources may have been through a slightly more formal publishing process than electronic ones, but there's still no substitute for finding the evidence that proves they can be relied upon. In any case, there's such a huge crossover between printed and electronic delivery now that the distinction between media no longer makes any sense in this context; the same document may well come out as a printed report, an e-book, a PDF that can be read on a computer, tablet or e-reader and an HTML file designed for a browser. In addition, electronic documents can be created by anyone at little or no cost, and it can be difficult to determine the relative status of different sources when they all come up as a homogeneous set of search engine results. So let's finish this chapter by looking at four specific types of source that you or your enquirer will probably need to evaluate especially carefully . . .

Blogs (short for 'weblogs') are online diaries that anyone can create and post on the web, using simple software. Their numbers are growing at an extraordinary rate and, by their very nature, they are completely uncontrolled. Some of the main search engines enable you to search blogs specifically. You can find blogs on the most esoteric of subjects, offering not only information but also the possibility of putting your enquirer in touch with a blogger who may be able to help them directly with their query. Obviously if you recognize a blogger as an acknowledged specialist in their field – one who contributes a regular column to a trade or professional journal, for example – then you can presumably trust the blog. If you can't be sure, then once again you need to assess the blogger's credentials, and probably double-check the blog's information elsewhere as well.

Microblogs are a subset of the genre. For technical reasons, these have a strict limit on the number of available characters per posting, so the information they contain is very compressed. They're also very quick and easy to write and publish, so they can represent off-the-cuff remarks that haven't necessarily been well considered. Social media services sometimes also accommodate microblogs as part of their offering, so don't ignore those as a possible source of such content. All the caveats that relate to blogs apply to microblogs too – but probably more so.

Wikis use special software to allow groups of people to contribute collaboratively to the same body of content and then edit or amend it. Wiki applications can appear on the web, where anyone could use them, or on a single organization's intranet, where they're only accessible to a closed group. Typical web applications include communal encyclopaedias, or services that allow whistleblowers to publish leaked documents anonymously. Conventional wisdom might suggest that wikis are inherently untrustworthy because anyone can amend them irrespective of their qualification to do so. However, they can also tend to be self-correcting, as errors or omissions may be quickly spotted by others and amended accordingly.

Open access is a movement among academics, researchers and professionals to make the full texts of their refereed articles and papers freely and permanently available online to anyone who wants to use them. There are two complementary forms of open access publishing. In one instance, authors can provide access to their own published articles, by making their electronic copies available free for all. Alternatively, journal publishers can provide free access to the articles – either by charging the author or institution for refereeing and publishing them (instead of charging the user for accessing them), or simply by making their online edition free for all. Governments and other official bodies that award grants for research are increasingly requiring the bodies they fund at public expense to publish their results free of charge online for anyone to access. So as the open access movement grows, it should result in more and more high-quality peer-reviewed content, whose reliability you can trust, being made available on the web.

Coming next – even more things that can go wrong

Smarter searching can help you stop a lot of things from going wrong and, as we've seen, can enable you to empower students or other library users whose researches you're guiding. But this isn't the only time when things can go awry. So in Chapter 5, we'll think about what to do when you're running out of time and still no nearer finding an answer. That's probably when you'll need to make good use of your lateral thinking skills.

To recap . . .

- **Enquirers have access to many of the same searching tools as you do – your job is to help them search smarter.**
- **Consider whether you need to use the most up to date, the most relevant or the most appropriate source before you start.**
- **Remember the pitfalls posed by variant spellings, homonyms and British versus American terminology.**
- **Where a search is likely to be complex or lengthy, construct your own mini-taxonomy before you start – and remember that all indexes, whether printed or electronic, have their limitations.**
- **Learn and practise strategic reading techniques, for when there's no index.**
- **Make sure that you can trust whatever you find.**
- **Above all, maximize your searching efficiency by thinking systematically.**

CHAPTER 5

Help! Everything's going wrong

Using lateral thinking to get out of difficulties

In this chapter you'll find out how to:

- **prioritize enquiries so the right ones get done first**
- **think of compromise solutions when time's running out**
- **decide what to do when you can't find the answer**
- **look for outside help**
- **exploit your lateral thinking skills.**

'The best laid schemes of mice and men gang aft agley', wrote the Scottish poet Robert Burns, musing on how easy it can be for things suddenly to go pear-shaped. How true! If you've stayed with us thus far your schemes will indeed have been 'best laid' ones. You'll have analysed the enquirer's needs to establish precisely what they want without any ambiguities, exercised your imagination to work out logically where the answer can be found, and searched systematically and professionally for the information you need. But you still can't find it, and time's running out.

It would be all too easy to feel the panic returning at a time like this. Enquirers really do think that the web has it all and you can get at it instantly, and that can trap you into agreeing to an unrealistic deadline despite your efforts to avoid it. So what you need to do is to manage their expectations while making sure you can deliver what you've promised – which is why it's so important to settle the matter of the deadline from the outset (as we discussed in Chapter 1).

But is the deadline always your problem? It clearly is if your job is to find information on behalf of other people. But what about when it's a student who's come to you with a really complex assignment which (as they so often seem to do) they've started far too late. Well, to be hard-nosed about it, you have two choices. You can tell them it's their problem and they should have thought of it sooner, leaving them to go off disgruntled with you and the library – or possibly to waste the time of a colleague on another desk in a different department.

Or you can demonstrate your professionalism in advising them what they can do in the limited time available, thereby casting yourself in the role of mentor rather than critic. To do this, you're now probably going to have to come at the problem sideways, thinking of ingenious alternative ways of tackling the enquiry that are no longer based on a logical linear progression from problem to solution. In other words, you're going to have to think laterally.

Vital versus urgent tasks

Before we get onto the ingenious stuff, though, let's go back to some of the basics of time management. You should find these useful in helping you organize your own work – whether enquiry-related or otherwise – and if you're able to instil the principles in the students or members of the public you help, then you'll be conferring a benefit on them too.

We discovered in Chapter 1 that 'urgent' is not an acceptable deadline for any enquiry. You need to know how urgent; you need a date and/or a time. Now we need to take that a stage further and make sure that we really understand what we mean by urgency. Faced with a limited amount of time and a number of competing tasks, you need first of all to sort them into priority order and allocate time between them – and you need to revise that timetable constantly as new tasks come along to demand your attention. To do this, you certainly need to be clear about how urgent each task that lies before you is – but, even more important, you also need to decide how vital it is to your organization.

Just as there are posh terms for your initial structured conversation with the enquirer (the 'reference interview' in Chapter 1 – remember?) and for imagining what the final answer will look like ('predictive search', in Chapter 3), so there's a posh term for this process too: triage. Usually applied to health care, it's the process of prioritizing patients to ensure that the ones with the severest conditions get treated first when resources are limited but that no one gets neglected altogether. But it's also used to prioritize business decisions, and problem solving in IT – and it's certainly applicable to enquiry handling.

Remember that in Chapter 1 we learned that 'urgent' was a useless way of specifying a deadline? Well it can actually be even worse than that, because 'urgent' is also a very emotive word that can induce panic and irrational decision making if you're not careful. Instead, it's far more helpful to decide whether a task is 'vital'. A **vital** task is one without which your organization can't function. An **urgent** task is one which has an imminent deadline; it may or may not be vital. Yet we often tend to be panicked by the idea of something being urgent without always considering the bigger question of how vital it is.

If you don't buy information sources, install, catalogue and index them, learn how they work, keep up payments on the subscription and upgrade them as required, then you can't answer the enquiries. So these are vital tasks. But they're not necessarily urgent; if you put them off until later, no great harm may be done. They may in due course become urgent. If you're constantly being asked for information that's sitting in a document that you haven't yet catalogued, or an application that you haven't yet installed or upgraded, or that's only available through a service where the subscription has lapsed, then fixing the problem becomes not only vital but also urgent. So it follows from this that the sensible way to prioritize your work is . . .

1 *Top priority:* Vital and urgent
2 *Followed by:* Vital but not yet urgent
3 *Then:* Theoretically urgent but actually not particularly vital
4 *And finally (if at all):* Neither vital nor urgent.

Now you might argue with the relative priority of items 2 and 3 and may want to reverse their order depending on the specific circumstances – but you get the principle. Now let's see how it might apply to enquiry work.

First come first served?

Let's say that you're a researcher with three urgent enquiries to do. They all have the same deadline. But one is for a colleague doing a college course on day release, another is for your boss and the third is for a client of your organization. Your job is to answer enquiries for all these three people, so they're all vital; if you don't do them, you'll be in trouble. But if you fail your colleague you'll probably just get ticked off; if you fail the boss you might lose your job; and if you fail the client, everyone might lose their jobs. So you can see that there are degrees of urgency, depending on how vital the task is. You might deal with this challenge by:

1 *First:* suggesting an appropriate source for the colleague to use for him or herself
2 *Second:* warning the boss that you're doing an enquiry for a client and either providing a brief holding answer for the boss or negotiating a longer deadline (or both); and then . . .
3 *Third:* concentrating on the client.

Once you've prioritized your competing enquiries in the manner outlined above, you can then work out how long you need to allocate to each. Five minutes with your catalogue or a couple of other finding aids may be enough for your college colleague, and 15 minutes looking up, downloading and e-mailing over a few pieces of information will put the boss on the back burner for a while. This leaves you the rest of the morning to spend doing database searches, scanning journal references and compiling a list of results for the client. (And preparing to present the answer in a helpful way; we'll look at different aspects of adding value in Chapters 6 and 7.)

Of course, it doesn't work like this in a busy public reference or college library. There every enquirer is equally important, and you have to employ different techniques to ensure that everyone's deadlines are met. To do this, you really need to be able to assess instantly the relative difficulty of answering each enquiry, and the amount of time you'll need to devote to it. There's probably no easy way of doing this; it comes with experience and, even then, you'll still encounter some enquiries that turn out to be almost impossible to answer, even though you thought they were going to be easy. But you can help yourself by making sure that you do know your basic reference sources really well – just a strictly limited number of them, such as some of the Starter Sources listed in Chapter 8 on Choosing Your Toolkit. If you are familiar with their contents, then you should know what's feasible and where you're going to have to negotiate with the enquirer about providing a compromise answer.

Time is money

Difficulty doesn't necessarily equate to time (although it might). An alternative to spending time trying to answer a difficult enquiry with the free web or available printed sources might be to use a charged-for database, where the time saved justifies the expense. Assuming that you've correctly identified the right one to use, fully searchable databases can save you an enormous amount of time – not least because they fail as quickly as they succeed. Just think about it for a moment. If you use printed sources or generic web search engines, it takes you longer to fail to find the answer than it does to succeed. That's because once you've found it you stop looking, whereas if you keep not finding it, you have to go on looking until you've exhausted every possibility.

However, if you've managed to locate the right specialist source – covering the right subject areas and offering sophisticated search functionality – that will fail as quickly as it succeeds. Why? Because, assuming you've framed your search appropriately (go back to Chapter 4 to check up on that), it will tell you instantly that there's nothing available on the subject – so you know much further ahead of the deadline that an enquiry is going to be difficult, and you still have time to do something about it.

The moral here is that time is money. Whether you choose to spend money on a charged-for search that takes five minutes, or restrict yourself to the free web or to available printed sources and spend an hour searching those instead, the result is the same – cost to your organization. In making efficient use of your time, and deciding when to call a halt and compromise on the answer instead, you must always bear in mind that every minute you spend on an enquiry is costing your organization money. It's not just the cost of your modest salary either, or the source's subscription price; there are overheads to take into account as well – things like lighting, heating, rent and property taxes, to say nothing of the cost of acquiring and managing all your information sources in the first place. The less efficiently you plan your search strategy, the more it costs your organization.

And while we're on the subject, there's a third resource that you can bring to bear here as well as time and money: your intellect. Deployed together in proportion, these three resources can actually determine how efficiently you carry out every task you undertake. We'll return to the business of ensuring that you're making best use of these three resources (Time, Intellect, Money – the TIM test, if you will) in Chapter 8.

Your working timetable

Back, meanwhile, to the challenges we're facing right now. We've already done some assessment of the relative difficulty of some of our sample enquiries in Chapter 3, by imagining what the final answer would look like, deciding what kinds of source would provide an answer that looked like that and determining the enquiry's viability in terms of the resources at our disposal. Assuming that they all have the same deadline (and that you do have access to all the sources necessary for answering them), let's go back to all the seven enquiries we started with in Chapter 1, assess them for how **easy** or **hard** they're likely to be, and whether they're likely to be **quick** or **slow** to complete.

Then we'll use these assessments to sort the enquiries into priority order for action, so that everybody gets started as quickly as possible. This means that you deal with the easiest and quickest enquiries first, rather than keeping people with simple enquiries waiting unnecessarily while you spend time on the slower and harder ones. On that basis, your assessment of each of these enquiries may come out as shown in the table below. (Check back to Chapter 1 for our analysis of each enquirer's actual requirements as shown here, and to Chapter 3 for what we imagined some of the final answers would look like.)

Enquiry	Easy/Hard	Quick/Slow
Do you have the electoral register?	Since this is actually a genealogical or ancestry query, not a simple request for the register, it's a bit less straightforward than might at first appear – but there are at least plenty of possible places to look, so this is pretty **easy** to get started on.	But identifying and searching through all the possible places – and probably discovering new ones along the way – could make it pretty **slow**.
I need: local newspaper reports about council questions on immigrants; information on the Strong & Moral Britain Association – especially its funding; and details of the obligations on school governors to declare other interests. And I don't want to use any online sources.	*The enquiry*: Since the enquirer has effectively forbidden use of the internet, this has turned a query that was always going to present its challenges into a very **hard** task. *The council questions*: Unless your enquirer can provide some pretty precise dates, finding the relevant ones is probably going to be **hard**. *The Association*: Few organizations can escape scrutiny on the web – especially potentially dubious ones like this one – so not being allowed to go online will probably make this aspect of the query **hard**.	*The enquiry*: Taking the three requests as a whole – and working on the principle that the speed of a convoy is the speed of its slowest vehicle – this enquiry could be very **slow**. *The council questions*: Finding them is likely to be a **slow** job using only printed sources (which are unlikely to be well indexed). *The Association*: You might have to try quite a few printed sources to get anything at all, which could make that job pretty **slow** too.

Enquiry	Easy/Hard	Quick/Slow
	The school governors: But you could argue that the only bit of this three-part query that really matters initially is what interests school governors have to declare. Even without using the web, that may prove quite **easy** to discover – with a bit of lateral thinking.	*The school governors*: The rules should be widely available – but the enquiry could be a bit **slow** to fulfil if you're not allowed to look them up online. So look out for ideas on compromise answers later in this chapter.
I'm doing a project on the Westminster Aquarium.	Since there's only a limited amount of available material, providing enough to enable the student to complete the assignment could be pretty **hard**.	Frustratingly coming up with the same limited material in all sorts of different sources is probably going to make it pretty **slow** as well.
I'm looking for information on migration patterns in Wales.	Fairly **easy** in that there are plenty of possible places to look – both for the raw figures and commentary on them.	But checking all those possible places will take time so it could end up being quite **slow**.
I'm looking for information on who's doing research into the health risks of artificial and natural radiation (and it's worth searching elsewhere if we don't find the article the enquirer thinks they remember from *New Scientist*).	Pretty **easy** in that there's no shortage of easily identifiable resources giving access to scientific literature.	Reasonably **quick** to get started, at least. But if the enquirer really wants comprehensive information on who's doing what, hunting enough material out to satisfy them could prove a bit **slow** in the long run.
I'm trying to find a song called *When I Would Sing Under the Ocean* [but the title is probably wrong].	Until you've found some way of discovering the real title, this enquiry will be extremely **hard**.	Coming up with a way of getting round this mystery could be a slow process. But if you can crack that and you do end up knowing the correct title, tracking the song down should be pretty **quick**.)
What is Marks & Spencer's current pre-tax profit?	Just a little bit of thought (or discussion with colleagues) should have suggested plenty of possible places to look, including simply going straight to the company's own website. So very **easy**.	Readily available on the web so – once you've worked out where to go – extremely **quick**.

Having done this triage-like assessment, we can now have a go at prioritizing these seven enquiries for action. The aim, remember, is to get everyone reading something at the earliest possible opportunity and not to have an Easy/Quick enquirer waiting around while you plough through a Hard/Slow query. So the results might come out like this . . .

Priority for action	Enquiry	Easy/Hard	Quick/Slow
1	Marks & Spencer's current pre-tax profit	**Easy**	**Quick**
2	Health risks of radiation	**Easy**	**Quick** to start **Slow** to complete
3	Migration patterns in Wales	Fairly **Easy**	Quite **Slow**
4	Electoral register [but there are better sources available for name searching]	Pretty **Easy**	Pretty **Slow**
5	Project on the Westminster Aquarium	Pretty **Hard**	Pretty **Slow**
6	Council questions on immigrants Strong & Moral Britain Association Rules for school governors [No online sources allowed]	*Whole enquiry*: Very **Hard** *Council questions*: **Hard** *Association*: **Hard** *School governors*: Potentially quite **Easy**	Whole enquiry: Very **Slow** *Council questions*: **Slow** *Association*: **Slow** *School governors*: A bit **Slow** (because you're not allowed to go online)
7	Song called *When I Would Sing Under the Ocean* [but the title is probably wrong]	Extremely **Hard**	**Slow** (until you know what the song is) **Quick** (once you know the correct title)

Beware, though! This sort of exercise can only ever be a rough guide to action – not the proverbial 'tablets of stone'. But if you're actually doing all the enquiries yourself, your chosen order of priority for action means that you can start getting answers out from the earliest possible moment, so no one has to wait longer than the difficulty or time-consuming nature of the enquiry merits. And if your job is to help the enquirers find the answers for themselves, then this strategy means that everyone gets started as rapidly as possible and you have time to monitor everybody's progress and help wherever necessary.

Of course, people's assessment of difficulty varies depending on their experience and the environment they work in; a music librarian might put the **Sing Under the Ocean** mystery right at the top of the list, for example, because at least they ought to be able to come up with plenty of ideas for tackling it. You may decide to split the secretive enquirer's query into three parts, dealing with the crucial bit – the rules for **school governors** – first; having discovered what the rules are, the enquirer may decide that they don't need to know the rest at all. And you probably won't discover that the

Westminster Aquarium query is going to take a long time until your enquirer is some way into it.

So you should take this section as a guide to the technique, not as the answer to the problem. It simply provides a working timetable for the order in which you get enquirers started; after that, as you perhaps start encountering unexpected difficulties in some of the enquiries, you'll probably need to deal with things on a first come first served basis.

Managing expectations

But, unfortunately, even this can't guarantee success. It may be that you really have more to do than you can possibly manage in the time available. In that case, you could find yourself having to compromise on the answer. Do avoid ever saying 'no' if you possibly can, but you have to accept that there will be times when you need to say 'yes – but . . . '. The important thing is to try to advance on all fronts – leave everybody with something, rather than some with a complete answer and others with nothing. There are various things you can do to keep to your deadlines.

Say 'no' positively

With so much information now available, in print, online and in electronic documents, is there any excuse for failing to find an answer? Sometimes. Your enquirer may decide that the information is just not worth the cost of using a charged-for service or hiring an independent information professional. You may decide that you can't afford to invest the time on a speculative and possibly fruitless attempt to find a source that might be able to help. No matter how much technology you surround yourself with, and no matter how well funded your organization, there are times when you might still have to admit defeat.

But even this doesn't mean saying 'no'. It means exercising ingenuity to help your enquirer to continue travelling hopefully instead of hitting a cul de sac. It means thinking laterally about what you can still do. Remember the technique you used when your mind went blank in Chapter 3? You said 'I'm sure I can help', and indeed you still can – although by now not necessarily in the way your enquirer expected. So what do you need to do next . . . ?

Prepare your enquirer for disappointment

First, it's probably just as well to start lowering your enquirer's expectations as soon as you realize there are going to be difficulties. Whether you've been advising the enquirer in their researches or actually doing the research yourself, it will certainly help if you've been keeping in regular touch with them. You'll be in a much better position to help them if they're already aware that you are having problems and are starting to think about what sort of alternative answer would do. In your dialogue with the enquirer at this stage, you again each have something to contribute. Your job is to say what's feasible, and your enquirer needs to say what's acceptable as an answer.

An enquirer who's there with you can probably see that things aren't going too well, but it's a bit more challenging if you have to deliver disappointing news remotely – by phone or e-mail for instance. As soon as they hear your voice, or see your message in their inbox, they're quite likely to assume that you're coming back with the answer – so you need to let them down gently. Try to have at least some positive news to deliver first – supply what little information you have been able to find, or at the very least report positively on where you've looked. And when you do come to break the bad news, try to couch it in terms of needing to consult the enquirer on how to carry the enquiry forward, rather than simply delivering the bald message that you can't find anything.

What you can do to save the situation at this stage will depend on what exactly your enquirer wants the information for. As we discovered in Chapter 1, people rarely want information merely to satisfy idle curiosity – they nearly always have a purpose in asking. This means that you can sometimes accommodate their needs by providing an alternative answer – less specific than the one they asked for, for example, but almost as helpful in enabling them to reach the outcome they seek. We'll come back to this in a moment – but what do you need to do in the meantime?

Ask for thinking time

You could try saying: 'Leave it with me a bit longer; I'll see what I can do.' This buys you valuable thinking time and leaves the enquirer satisfied that you are taking the enquiry seriously. However, you must take the time straight away to go again through the full questioning procedure that we discussed in Chapter 1, based on what you now know about the difficulty of the task – particularly the Why? and How? of the enquirer's reasons for asking the question in the first place. You must also agree a new deadline with the enquirer – and then meet it. But what are we going to do with this thinking time? Two possibilities: Come up with a Plan B for answering the enquiry in-house; or referring it elsewhere. Either of these options could involve a healthy dose of lateral thinking. We'll look at both in just a moment.

Provide progress reports

Whatever strategies you choose to employ to ensure you still meet your deadlines despite your new-found difficulties, it's important to keep enquirers informed about how you're getting on. It's reassuring to the enquirer, and it shows them that you're being open about the difficulties and not trying to pull the wool over their eyes. Although you'll always hope to succeed, progress reports can also prepare enquirers for ultimate disappoint-ment (and put them in a mood for accepting a compromise answer) if your searching continues to go badly. You're likely to do this automatically when the enquirer is standing over you, but you should get into the habit of doing it for absent enquirers too. Whether you're delivering good news or bad, making progress reports may seem irksome and time-consuming, but it undoubtedly pays customer relations dividends.

Plan B

Although we've drawn a blank at every turn so far, it's by no means the end of the road. However, you are now probably going to have to rethink the task and discuss alternative strategies with your enquirer. Sometimes you can anticipate this difficulty. So what are the options . . . ?

Offer a rough-and-ready answer

If you've just asked for more thinking time (see above), that merely leaves you with yet another deadline to meet. So an alternative tactic might be to offer an instant but partial answer, based on what you have immediately to hand. (This tactic works equally well whether the enquirer is standing in front of you or has got in touch using a remote medium.) A rough-and-ready answer is usually a briefer one – whatever you can find in a few minutes in readily accessible sources. However, there are some occasions when a rough-and-ready answer can be a longer one. It might take only a few minutes to do a quick search and hand the results over unchecked for the enquirer to go through in detail in their own time. But if it's normally your job to actually do the research, you may also want to offer to go through the downloaded results yourself later, removing less relevant material and drawing attention to the best sources, when time allows. (Appraising search results, and presenting them in the most helpful way for your enquirer's purposes, is all part of adding value, and we'll return to this aspect of it in Chapter 7.)

Suggest a compromise answer

If neither you nor your enquirer can find any sources that provide the complete answer required, and your deadline is looming, now's the time to start considering a compromise answer – one that's less detailed or less up to date than the enquirer would ideally like. But this must be a joint decision between you and the enquirer with (as we've seen earlier) you saying what's feasible and the enquirer saying what's acceptable. Let's think about possible compromise answers to a couple of our sample enquiries.

There just might not be enough time to undertake a full analysis of all the **migration figures for Wales** from the mass of statistical data available online. So will the enquirer settle for a pre-packaged digest of the headline figures from the relevant government agency, ready to download in a spreadsheet, plus a handful of articles that explain the trends in brief? You may have been the one to find this material, but it's for the enquirer to say whether it will do in the circumstances.

The student doing the **Westminster Aquarium** enquiry may simply not have found enough material to sustain their project, but in their searching they should at least have encountered a great deal of tangential material along the way. So is this the time for them to return to their tutor and negotiate a change in the brief – broadening it out, perhaps, to put the Aquarium in the context of other forms of popular Victorian entertainment, on which plenty of material should by now be available? Or if there isn't time to do this – students so frequently only seem to come to the library when their deadline is looming – can you both at least revisit the reading list associated with the project, and try to deduce from the titles listed there what might be an acceptable way of extending the brief.

And although the enquirer about **immigration questions** and a **neo-fascist Association** might be extremely anxious about using the internet, it might still be possible to persuade them that finding out about rules for school governors is such a normal and uncontroversial enquiry that nothing untoward could come from putting that part of the enquiry, at least, to the web. It may even be that, once they've had a chance to study the rules about declarations of interest, they realize that they don't need to pursue the other aspects of the enquiry at all.

But beware! Whatever you decide to do at this stage of any enquiry, you've changed the agenda to suit yourself. So be especially sensitive to your enquirer's reaction, to make sure that the suggested change also suits them. Your enquirer will not be impressed if you try to present a less than satisfactory answer as a lovely surprise.

Suggest sources rather than finding answers

Suggesting sources in which your enquirer can look, rather than finding the answer for them, is an obvious tactic, and face-to-face enquirers will probably be sympathetic if they can see that you're under pressure from other people standing round. If you do suggest sources to an enquirer who's actually with you, make sure that you explain fully how the source works; show them the different indexes available in a printed source, take them through the various menus or buttons on a website or in an electronic document. And invite them to return for further advice if the source doesn't work; don't ever give the impression that you're fobbing them off.

It can be a lot harder to convince an enquirer that you're short of time if there's no one else around, no matter how many jobs you are working on for absent enquirers – and this tactic may be of no help at all to a remote enquirer, who's contacted you precisely because they can't get access to the specialist sources that you will be using.

Always keep an eye out for better sources

Whether you're doing the research yourself or supporting others in their researches, it's always a good idea to scrutinize any bibliographies you find in the publications you do try, or any promising looking links on the websites you visit. They may lead you to more detailed sources that your enquirer might be able to see in a specialist library or borrow through a document supply service. Exploiting bibliographies in this way can be an incredibly efficient way of finding the specialist sources you need to enable you to satisfy your enquirer's needs precisely – and, if you're supporting students, it's also a really good practice to inculcate in them.

Referrals

We've probably now reached the stage where we've exhausted all the resources we could draw upon in-house (including the free web, of course). But seeking outside help usually imposes delays on the answer and there will be occasions when you don't realize that you're in difficulties until the deadline is looming.

So before you take that decision, do have one final check to make sure you really have exhausted all the in-house possibilities. If you're in a public library, is there a more experienced colleague who happens to be working in a back office at the moment, or a specialist at a bigger branch, whose brains you might be able to pick? If you're helping a student or academic in a college library, have you contacted the relevant library subject specialist, who may only occasionally take turns on the desk but is otherwise on call to assist with tricky enquiries within their particular discipline?

If it's a student, can they go back to their tutor for further guidance at this stage – including discussing whether the assignment is realistic at all? And if you're a researcher in a specialist organization, are you sure you've tapped all the available in-house expertise away from your own information centre? (And do you have know-how files to help you to do this? We'll come back to those in Chapter 8.)

Assuming you've done all those final checks, you probably have no option left other than to look elsewhere. You may even be able to judge by now that the enquiry is so esoteric and so specific that the answer might not be in a published source at all, and that locating expert advice is the only solution. If so, this is the time when you need to bring in the fourth characteristic that we considered in Chapter 3 in addition to focus, dynamism and complexity: viability. At this late stage, what could make the enquiry viable?

Ask authors or editors

Whether you're doing the searching yourself or advising a student in their researches, it's a really good idea to keep a note of the authors of nearly relevant books, articles or (expert) blogs, or the editors of what seem like appropriate journals (whether printed or web-based). So even if you draw a blank with the documents you scrutinize, you still have the option of contacting an author or editor in the hope that they can advise you on more specialized sources.

For reasons we've already discussed in Chapter 4, it's almost certainly best to use a professionally edited source to find those authors if you can, rather than just going blindly onto the web. There are plenty of Who's Who-type publications that cover writers, but the trouble is that sources of this kind are always highly selective in who they include, and aren't necessarily particularly up to date. Alternatively you (or the enquirer) could try using a social networking site to locate the authors you need – but in this case you always run the risk that you're just one among thousands of followers and that your request never attracts the author's attention.

So another way might be to use the book's publisher as a go-between. Actually this isn't an ideal solution either, because professional authors (as opposed to enthusiasts) are often reluctant to enter into correspondence, and publishers tend to be protective of their authors too. It partly depends on what kind of author it is. If it's a jobbing writer who makes their living from churning out non-fiction books they're unlikely to be very keen to help. But if it's a specialist in the relevant field – an academic, say – they might be much more willing to advise. Contacting authors of articles in specialist journals or blogs, or the editors of those journals or blogs, can be more fruitful. Driven by their own enthusiasm, they may be more committed to their subject than a commercial writer or publisher would be.

Suggest alternative libraries or information services

As we've already established, suggesting sources doesn't necessarily work with remote enquirers. And, as we saw in Chapter 2, it can be well nigh impossible to contain a remote enquirer's impatience, no matter how busy you are. So if you can't help them immediately, you could suggest an alternative library or information service that they could try. But again, be as helpful as possible in doing this. Look up the organization's phone number, e-mail address and website, and tell your enquirer exactly what that service can do that you can't. In some cases, merely giving an e-mail enquirer the web address of a relevant institution may be sufficient in itself – especially if its site has a good Frequently Asked Questions (FAQs) section. Beware, though, of directing enquirers to services that they are not entitled to use. Some institutions will accept enquiries only from their members or subscribers; others will want to charge.

Look for other forms of outside help

If you've got to this stage and you're still stuck for a solution, then it's probably time to seek other forms of outside help. There are plenty of possible sources that can help you with this, and you will be very unlucky indeed if you can't find anywhere at all to direct your enquirer to. (Have a look at some of the Starter Sources featured in Chapter 8; many of them can lead you to further sources of help.) Seeking outside help does have the advantage of sticking to the enquirer's agenda, whereas if you suggest a substitute answer, you inevitably shift the agenda to suit you. But – besides the delay – going outside may mean that you can no longer necessarily guarantee the attention and courtesy that you are, of course, giving your own enquirer.

So if you do decide that you need to seek outside help, how do you decide where to go? We've already seen how imagining the final answer can get you started on possible sources to try. Now, faced with the task of referring the enquiry somewhere else, there's another hypothetical question you need to ask yourself – and this time it's . . .

Who really needs to know this?

In other words, what kind of organization just couldn't function if it didn't have the information that you need? Whose job would be on the line if they couldn't tackle an enquiry like this? That's the sort of contact you need to locate, and finding one can frequently be pretty straightforward; you have the subject of the enquiry so you just need to look up an organization that specializes in it. But there are some occasions where you have to exercise a little lateral thinking in determining what kind of organization or person that might be – and you may also need to be a bit cautious about how you handle what they provide.

So, with those warnings, let's see how the technique might work for you with some of the most intransigent of our sample enquiries.

Problematic enquiry	Who really needs to know this?	Caveat
I'm doing a project on the Westminster Aquarium.	By now the student should at least have discovered exactly where the building was. In response, you will probably be aware – or could speculate – that the local studies library, archive or record office for the area concerned may well be able to provide more detailed material from their original records.	Even a specialist local organization may not be able to provide a sufficient quantity of additional original or primary source material to satisfy the student's needs. So it may still be necessary for the student to go back to their tutor and renegotiate the terms of the assignment.

Problematic enquiry	Who really needs to know this?	Caveat
Can you confirm whether the Strong & Moral Britain Association is linked with neo-fascist organizations?	If it's the kind of organization your enquirer suspects, then it probably won't be particularly forthcoming with information about itself – either in any publication or if you try to phone on the enquirer's behalf and ask it directly. But working on the principle of 'Know thine enemy', the kind of organization that would really need to know about an outfit like this would be one that was opposed to it – so try looking for anti-fascist or anti-racist organizations, or equality bodies that might be able to advise you.	Even though the organization you decide to contact for advice may be well regarded and have laudable aims, it will still nevertheless have its own agenda to pursue. So when you report back, you should make clear to your enquirer what the aims, objectives and values of the organization you contacted are. (Try their About Us web page for this.)
I'm trying to find a song called *When I Would Sing Under the Ocean* [but the title is probably wrong].	Logically, nobody *really needs* to know this song title because it doesn't exist. So you're going to have to rely on someone, somewhere, making an intuitive leap and working out what the correct title is likely to be. A light opera or musical enthusiast might be the kind of person you need – and that could include the author of a guide to the subject or, indeed, many knowledgeable music librarians. So, to increase the odds of finding that special person, why not crowdsource it? It only takes one knowledgeable person out of potentially thousands on a relevant discussion list or social network to work out that the song is probably *When I Was King of the Boeotians* from Offenbach's *Orpheus in the Underworld*.	Your knowledgeable contact has certainly unblocked the enquiry, giving you a fresh avenue to pursue, and you would of course be very grateful to them for that. But you haven't yet answered the enquiry. You now need to find a copy of the song (in whatever medium the enquirer is seeking) and check with them that it is indeed what they were looking for. Also, beware of using crowdsourcing too often. You don't want to get a reputation for being too lazy to tackle your own enquiries!

Having found what looks like the right organization to help, there's still no guarantee that it will co-operate. So keep your request sensible – ask for only the minimum amount of help you need in order to move forward. It also helps if you can avoid the telephone merry-go-round that you risk encountering if you simply phone the organization's switchboard. So try using some of the Starter Sources detailed in Chapter 8 on Choosing Your Toolkit to see first if an organization has a library or information service, where you could reasonably expect a more sympathetic response than you might get from the reception desk. Failing that, see if the organization has a public relations department – the bit that's paid to be nice to outsiders. Above all, if your enquirer is planning to visit the organization, do prepare the ground for them; don't just send them off on a wild goose chase. If they do try somewhere else on your recommendation and get a dusty answer in response, that will reflect badly on you.

Buy the information in

Realistically, purchasing the information your enquirer needs, as opposed to finding it within resources that you already have, is rarely a viable option. But it would be unwise to rule it out altogether. Many library users are accustomed to the idea of paying a modest charge to get hold of a licensed copy of a crucial journal article, for example. Or an academic with a research grant for the project they're working on may have been required to reserve some part of that money specifically for information purchase. And if your job is to undertake research on behalf of a specialist organization, then using a commercial database with a corporate credit card, or even employing an independent specialist information professional, may be more cost-effective than simply carrying on searching through ever less and less likely sources in the hope of achieving a breakthrough.

Of course, if you find yourself regularly having to buy in information to meet the needs of particular enquirers, that's the time to consider whether you shouldn't instead be investing in your own resources to meet what is clearly an ongoing requirement. (More on this in Chapter 6.) These are also crucial decisions that you will have to take when you're initially planning the kind of enquiry service most appropriate for your organization. (We'll return to that in Chapter 8.)

Coming next – adding value

Let's continue on a more positive note. This book is about success, after all. But successful enquiry answering doesn't simply mean handing the answer over with no further comment. It's about making sure that what you provide is the best available, presented to your enquirer in the most helpful way possible. So in the next couple of chapters, we'll look at how you can use your creative and critical thinking skills to add value to your answers.

To recap . . .

- **Distinguish between vital and urgent tasks.**
- **Prioritize your enquiries on the easy/hard quick/slow principle.**
- **Make sure that any compromise solution really meets your enquirer's needs.**
- **If you're not sure where to go for help, ask yourself who really needs to know it.**
- **When you're stuck on an enquiry, that's the time to exercise your lateral thinking skills.**

CHAPTER 6

Success! Now let's add some value

Using your creative thinking skills to present your answer well

In this chapter you'll find out how to:

- **quality check your answer**
- **present it effectively orally, in writing or visually**
- **make sure you've observed copyright and licensing requirements**
- **confirm that the enquirer is satisfied**
- **gather performance data**
- **use your creative thinking skills to enhance your service.**

'It ain't what you do, it's the way that you do it,' goes the old Ella Fitzgerald song. True enough – but the real wisdom is in the last line: 'That's what gets results'.

Whether you're helping members of the public, mentoring students or providing a full research service to a specific organization, there's every reason to take pride in the answers you provide. This is partly for your personal satisfaction, but it's also really good customer relations. A service that looks and sounds good inspires customer confidence and wins repeat business; one that doesn't risks losing that confidence, resulting in declining business and possibly even closure. In helping people find the information they want, you haven't been doing something easy, you've been doing something highly skilled – so don't spoil it with a weak finish.

Obviously, presenting your answer well matters when you're providing finished research results. (We're going to look at this in more detail in Chapter 7.) But it's just as important to be clear and concise – and to prioritize the information you provide – when you're advising enquirers on sources or search techniques. Presentation also matters when you're advising on a transaction such as how to request a document, access an electronic resource, use an online service or follow a procedure. Whatever the circumstances, presentation isn't an optional extra; it's an essential ingredient for the future development of your service. To achieve it, you need to be able to think creatively.

Quality-checking your answer

But just before you present your answer, it's wise to have one final quality check – just to make sure you haven't missed anything important or accidentally done something silly. As with so many of these stages in the enquiry-answering process, it may seem a bit tedious – but it's far better if you discover a howler before delivering the answer rather than letting the enquirer find it afterwards. So a few thoughts on final things to check . . .

Have you really answered it?

Remember that you have an implied contract with your enquirer as a result of all the careful questioning you undertook at the start of the process. So now go back and check the recorded wording of the enquiry carefully. Do this for two reasons – first, because you waste your enquirer's time if you find that you've allowed yourself to be unconsciously diverted during the course of your researches. Printed and electronic sources are full of diverting side alleys, and you need to be sure that you haven't been tempted. Second, you need to check because enquirers are quite capable of changing the agenda while you are searching without bothering to tell you. Remember the problems we encountered in Chapter 1, trying to find out what the enquirer really wanted in the first place? Unfortunately, it doesn't stop there. While you are busy trying to find the answer, your enquirer is still thinking about the question, and probably coming up with all sorts of supplementary information that they'd like as well. Or they may have been pursuing their own researches in parallel to yours, and have already come up with the answer themselves. Annoying as this may be, you have to be tolerant. After all, it's just a job for you, but it might be personally very important to them.

What to leave out – what to keep in

We worried about providing too much information as early as Chapter 1. But it's now, while you're preparing to present your answer, that this really matters. You may well have found similar information in several different sources. This could be because you were unhappy with the level of detail or reliability of the first source you used, and wanted to see whether you could improve on it in another one. Or because you found several articles or news items on the same subject, with huge overlaps between them. Alternatively, you might have located half a dozen different organizations that you could refer your enquirer to, because you haven't been able to find the information in-house.

But there's no rule that says you have to supply them all. As the quantity of available information continues to grow, enquirers will be looking to library and information professionals for their expertise not only in finding the right answer but also in judging which is the best version of the right answer. All information work is about choices – choosing what sources to buy, choosing what index entries to create for them, choosing what to leave out when you write abstracts of them. Why should enquiry work be any different?

So what sorts of things do you need to consider when deciding what to keep in your final answer? Here are a few quality indicators that you could use:

- **Is the information true?** It may seem obvious, but confirming the truth of what you intend to provide is more important than ever now that anyone can publish anything on the web – including deliberate falsehoods. So – particularly if the information looks way out of line, or even too good to be true – do make sure you investigate the source carefully.
- **Is the source authoritative?** Who is the author? If it's an individual, do they appear to be appropriately qualified in the subject and to have followed a relevant career path? If it's an organization, what kind is it? Is it official, regulated or a centre of excellence?
- **What is the source's agenda?** It's probably fair to say that all information reflects the author's values, which will in turn dictate what they've chosen to emphasize or ignore, whether that author is an individual or an organization. So are you satisfied that you understand what the author's agenda is, and are you ready to explain that to the enquirer – based on the facts, not your own value judgement?
- **Have you seen it referred to several times already?** Has the same source come up in different bibliographies, retrieved database records or search engine results? (Actually, as we've seen in Chapter 4, this is no longer

necessarily a foolproof test. The web is a viral medium and it may be that the same misleading document has been copied from location to location to location unchecked. So you do need to satisfy yourself about the source's authority and agenda as well.)

- **Will it allow your enquirer to . . .** reach a decision, make a recommendation or take action? As we've already seen in Chapter 1, enquirers usually ask for information for a specific purpose, not merely to satisfy idle curiosity. So you do need to ensure that what you intend to provide really will meet the enquirer's practical requirements.

Information versus references

Of course, there will be times when you genuinely don't feel qualified to make decisions of this kind – in highly specialized subjects such as medicine or law, for instance. But even then you can still opt for offering complete texts of only some of the sources, and providing references to the others. (More about this in Chapter 7.) That way, you've minimized the amount that your enquirer has to read and, if you're providing your answer on paper, then you've also been kind to trees.

Whatever you finally decide to provide, you should always tell your enquirer where the information has come from. It may be tempting to keep these details to yourself, in a misguided attempt to ensure that the enquirer remains dependent on you. But resist the temptation. First, it's a very unprofessional practice for one whose job is providing information from third-party sources. Second, it's all too easy for an enquirer to go to another library or information service that is prepared to source its information. And third, if your enquirer subsequently comes back for further details, it's extremely embarrassing if you can't remember where the information came from in the first place.

Presenting your answer – orally

Now you're finally ready to present it. So just take a few moments to decide how you're going to do that. After all, you don't want to spoil the climax, do you?

Preparing your answer

You may think that presenting an answer orally is just like normal conversation and doesn't need any prior preparation. Well, it isn't and it does. An oral answer needs to be as carefully structured and as clearly laid out as a written one. It's quite likely, for instance, that your enquirer will be taking notes while you deliver your oral answer, so it's only sensible to make their note-taking as easy as possible by setting out your message logically. If you're responding by phone, remember too that it will probably take a few seconds for the person at the other end to get onto your wavelength. So use those seconds to introduce yourself, say where you're calling from and remind the enquirer what they asked for. Then check that they're ready to take the information down. Then give them the answer.

There are a couple of storytelling techniques that might help you to do this. The first is the one beloved of trainers: tell them what you're going to tell them; tell them; then tell them what you've told them. And the second technique is one that journalists classically use: the inverted pyramid. When you read a detective novel, you want the apex of the pyramid – who did it – to be kept back to the very last page. But when you read a news story, you want the *denouement* to come first. So a news story will start with the climax, then give important supporting detail and finally include less relevant ancillary information at the bottom. This is so a reader can leave the story at any point, satisfied that they have the most important information, and it also enables an editor to chop off a story for length at the bottom, secure in the knowledge that they haven't excised anything important. Either of the two techniques shown can be useful for delivering oral answers – so let's see how they both might work if you were phoning through the answer to the very simple enquiry 'What is Marks & Spencer's current pre-tax profit?'

First of all using the **Tell them . . .** technique:

Introduce yourself . . .	Hello, is that Mr Sampson? This is Delilah Milton from the Ghaza Mills Library.
Tell them what you're going to tell them . . .	You asked me to find Marks & Spencer's current pre-tax profit, and I have the information for you if you're ready.
Tell them . . .	The current figures come from their full year results, published on 25 May and show results for the 53 weeks to 16 April. The underlying profit before tax is given as £689.6 million and the profit before tax as £488.8 million. However they also give figures for the 52 weeks to 26 March, and those figures are £684.1 million and £483.3 million respectively.
Tell them what you've told them . . .	So just to confirm, there are four headline figures this time, published in a press release on the company's website on the day the results came out.

Give the enquirer a chance to respond . . .	Is there anything else I can help you with at this stage?
And add some value . . .	Would you like me to text or e-mail those figures over to you?
	And do you need an explanation of why they additionally quote underlying results?
	The release includes other headline figures and comparisons with the previous period. Would it help if I sent you the web address of the release, so you can extract whatever other figures you might need?

Using this technique, you can confine your actual answer to the specific piece of information the enquirer asked for, while making certain at the same time that they really have taken that information in. But what happens to all the other related information that the enquirer didn't ask for but which you will inevitably have discovered at the same time? Using the Tell them . . . technique you can at least offer it without necessarily having prepared it in advance. But with the inverted pyramid technique you need to have all the available information ready to report straight away, and allow the enquirer to cut you off once they have enough.

So now the same answer using the **inverted pyramid**. Again you'd introduce yourself, to give the enquirer an opportunity to gather their thoughts. After that, your oral report might go like this . . .

Climax	The Marks & Spencer Group's profit before tax, which you asked for, is currently £488.8 million. The company explains that it has reached this figure by taking the underlying profit before tax, which is £689.6 million, and subtracting non-underlying items totalling £200.8 million.
	This is from the company's own full year results, covering the 53 weeks to 16 April, published in a press release on its website on 25 May. But it also gives figures for the 52 weeks to 26 March, which are £483.3 million and £684.1 million – again with the £200.8 million subtracted.
	Would you like a bit more detail about these figures?
Supporting information	The company explains that underlying results are consistent with how business performance is measured internally, and that the non-underlying items principally include: the mis-selling provision for M&S Bank; one-off impairments within M&S International; and UK store review costs and asset write-offs of IT.
	There's also an explanation of why they give figures for 53 weeks as well as 52, if you'd like to hear it?

Ancillary information	In its full annual report, which was published on the web at the same time as the press release, the company explains that it includes an additional week every six years to ensure that the year-end date stays in line with the end of March. But it adds that, in order to provide meaningful comparison with the previous year's 52-week period, it reports all financial movements on a 52-week basis, excluding the 53rd week, unless otherwise noted.
	The full report includes other profit figures as well – for M&S UK, M&S International and the M&S Bank – and other performance information, too, for individual Divisions such as Clothing and Food.
	Would it help if I sent you the web address where can find all this information, in case you'd like to study it further for yourself?

As before, you'd give the enquirer a chance to respond – but this time you'd pause at each step in the pyramid, giving them exactly the same opportunity to stop you as the reader of a news story has. You may of course argue that the enquirer didn't ask for all this ancillary stuff. But it does offer useful information as to why the figures are as they are, and it's all part of adding value to your answer – if the enquirer wants it.

Two final points. First, although in this instance you didn't offer to supply the web address until the end, you did give the source of the information right at the beginning. As with any enquiry work, the source of your information isn't an ancillary detail; it's part of the climax. And second you may recall that, when we were imagining the final answer to this enquiry (in Chapter 3), we decided that we would be looking for a single monetary figure of recent date. As it turned out, the answer that we eventually found was a little more complex than that. But we still found it exactly where we anticipated we would – on the company's own website.

Recommending sources or search strategies

These two techniques – Tell them . . . and the inverted pyramid – work just as effectively when you're delivering information face to face. And they also work when you're supporting students or members of the public in their searching as opposed to doing the actual research for them. With the Tell them . . . technique, you may decide to begin by outlining all the available sources to use, then explain in a little more detail what each of these sources will do, and finally review them, perhaps with a recommendation on the best sources to try first. Using the inverted pyramid, you might begin by recommending a couple of the best sources, then outline the ones to turn to next if necessary, and finally list the others that you don't recommend. (There are also more story-telling techniques in Chapter 7.)

Giving instructions

If ever there were a time when you needed to plan your oral delivery of information carefully, it's when you're giving instructions – how to reserve a book, order an electronic article, pay a fine, navigate through a portal or round a discovery tool, set up a feed, use an advanced search engine, understand the structure of a website. It's not too bad when the enquirer is with you, and you can watch over their shoulder and take them through the process one stage at a time. But it's much trickier when you're trying to guide them by phone. So here are some things to think about.

First of all, take everything step by step; don't be tempted to give more than one instruction at a time. Instead, give the first instruction, tell the enquirer what should happen as a result, and wait until they've confirmed that it has. Of course, that assumes that what you expect to happen actually does happen. If the enquirer says that it hasn't, you're flying blind because you can't see what's come up on their screen and it can take ages to find out what's caused the problem.

So a better technique is to do the task yourself while explaining how to do it – right up to the point where the enquirer needs to put in their actual request. That way you won't accidentally miss a step out and – hopefully – if something does go wrong it will go wrong on your screen as well as the enquirer's, at the same point in the process. However, you do need to make sure that you and the enquirer are starting at the same place; so if necessary, send them the address of the page where you want to start. Obviously while you're instructing the enquirer you'll be using your own user ID and password and the enquirer will be using theirs; so it's important to ensure that your personal identifier as a member of staff doesn't mean that you can see things on the screen that the enquirer can't or that you go through stages that the enquirer doesn't. But if you still suspect that you and the enquirer are not looking at the same thing – using different browsers, for example – you can ask the enquirer to send you a screenshot so you can see where the problem lies. (And you may have to instruct them in how to do that too.)

Presenting your answer – in writing

Everything that we discussed about presenting answers orally applies to written answers too – only more so. The enquirer can't interrupt and query things so easily in writing – even when you're using a comparatively interactive medium like texting or instant messaging – because it takes time to type a response and that interrupts the flow of the conversation. So it's important to compose your written answer carefully, using the same storytelling techniques that we looked at earlier and trying to anticipate the points at which the enquirer might raise queries. Let's think about what this might mean for the various ways in which you could deliver written information.

E-mail

E-mail is probably the commonest medium you'll use to deliver written answers, and it has a lot going for it. There are no restrictions on the length of an e-mail and it's easy to include links and attachments within it. Whether received on a desktop computer, laptop or tablet device, e-mails should be easy to read, with enough text showing in each screenful for the enquirer to be able to take in the totality of the answer comparatively easily. But bear in mind that your enquirer might receive the e-mail on a smartphone or other small-screen device – so it may help them to read it more easily if you keep your paragraphs short.

E-mail is a relatively informal medium, so it also helps if you keep e-mails friendly. There's a good practical reason for this: you're much less likely either to cause or take offence if you keep your wording conversational. So avoid using formal language in your e-mails and your pre-composed e-mail responses. A more relaxed, conversational style is generally more appropriate, although you may have to develop policies with your management on what degree of informality is acceptable. It's also a good idea to avoid using passive constructions in e-mails; they can come across as bureaucratic and inflexible. And if you do have to deliver disappointing news by e-mail, try to start with a possible solution to the problem. Finally, just before you send it, say it in your head. Are you certain that the enquirer isn't going to interpret it as being unsympathetic or unhelpful, or as you doing a 'job's worth'? Remember the message in Chapter 2: it's the recipient who decides where to place the emphasis on the words you send – not you.

Attachments

An e-mail with an attachment can often constitute the perfect answer to an enquiry: a report on what you've done and what you've found, backed up by the documentary evidence to support it. But don't assume that your enquirer has ultra-fast broadband. They may be using a mobile internet connection at a comparatively slow speed, or be in a rural area where broadband service is unreliable – or even still be on dial-up. So check first if it's OK to include an attachment, tell them what the file size is, and see if it isn't possible to send them a link instead.

Enhancing electronic documents

With information presented electronically, the number of ways you can enhance it is only limited by your own imagination. If you're sending a **word-processed document**, you can help your enquirer to make sense of a large body of text by adding headlines, subheadings and guiding, and by highlighting the key words or phrases in the text in bold or italic. Finding those words or phrases is easy for you; using the word search facility in your word-processing package or web browser, it takes only a few seconds for you to add an enormous amount of value to the answer. Alternatively, you could copy key paragraphs out of the original text and paste them in at the head of your answer. This allows your enquirer to take in the crucial information immediately, and to read it in its proper context later on – a variant of the inverted pyramid technique.

You can enhance **numeric data** in the same way. If you have downloaded some statistical information to a spreadsheet, then it need be the work of only a few minutes to add value by calculating an average or median for the figures retrieved, or expressing them as percentages for greater clarity, or ranking them. Or you can turn them into a graph, bar or pie chart, usually using software embedded within the spreadsheet package. Make sure you really understand what you're doing, though. It's all too easy for simple mistakes in spreadsheet creation to render figures seriously misleading, if not downright wrong.

As we saw in Chapter 3, **images** are now an immensely valuable source of information. So you can drop images into word-processed documents, or even supply your answer as a presentation, an infographic or a web page if you think that's more appropriate. And as with electronic text, you don't always need to show the whole picture; if one detail is particularly important, crop it out of the main image using standard image-processing software or even simply the image-formatting facility on your word processor or presentation package. (But see also the section on copyright later in this chapter. If you intend to source other people's images using the major search engines, it's worth filtering your search by 'usage rights' or 'licence' – the terminology varies from one search engine to another – to help you determine what you're allowed to do with what you find.)

If you're sending **PDF documents**, which you can't easily edit without the right software, you can at least copy key elements – whether text or images – out of the original and paste them into your covering e-mail with appropriate comment.

Two words of warning before you do any of this, though. Make sure your enquirer is fully aware of how your enhanced versions of documents differ from the original – and of course bear in mind that there may be important copyright and licensing limitations that you need to be aware of. (We'll return to these issues later in the chapter.)

Texting

Using the Short Message Service (SMS) on a mobile phone – texting – can be a very effective way of communicating. It's a one-to-one medium that many enquirers, especially students, tend to use heavily and trust, and it can be very user-friendly if used sensitively – so it's potentially good for customer relations. But it imposes limits on how much you can say in so many ways.

Individual SMS messages can be up to 160 characters in length. That's roughly about 26 words (including spaces and punctuation), or perhaps 2–3 sentences. However, it is possible for most phones to break up longer text messages into segments and send them in sequence for the receiving device to reassemble at the other end. In practice, 6–8 segments is the maximum, and since you need part of the message space for the data to enable the receiving device to reassemble the message correctly, this reduces the available number of message characters in each segment to around 150 or less. It means that you can send up to about 900–1200 characters in a 'concatenated' text message, or very roughly 150–200 words – assuming that your enquirer's device can accept and process messages sent in segments, that is.

On older conventional mobile phones you can rarely see more than about three lines of text at a time and three to four words per line – less if you use long words. You can see a lot more text on smartphones with bigger screens.

But it still only amounts to a medium-length paragraph per screen, with not more than about seven words per line if the recipient can't reorientate their screen to receive text in 'landscape' form (i.e. wider than it is high). With any kind of small screen, the enquirer can't rely so much on their peripheral vision to take in the whole message and may have to remember the earlier part of a lengthy message while reading the later part. Finally, the characters are quite small and SMS messages tend to come out as a single block of text, so they can sometimes be difficult to read and understand easily and quickly.

However, there are things you can do to overcome some of these limitations. First, keep your sentences and your words as short as possible. (This is actually good practice no matter how you choose to communicate.) Also, don't include more information than you could reasonably put in a single short paragraph of around two to three sentences. Make sure the message is easily understandable, written in plain language and clearly structured. If you have to send web addresses using SMS, shorten them using one of several available shortening tools, both to save your limited message space and to avoid blocking several lines on a tiny screen with a lengthy address. Yet, despite the space limitations, try not to make your messages too terse. Reserve some space for a friendly greeting and sign-off if you can. Having said that, though, it's probably not a good idea to use other compressions (e.g. cul8r – 'see you later'); you can't be certain the recipient will know what they mean.

Other, less formal, communication media

Social media now provide so many means of communicating both text and images that you're probably going to need to decide on which of these you intend to have a presence. Whichever of these services you decide to use, the same considerations are likely to apply as with SMS when it comes to things like brevity and clarity. Whatever their individual technical limitations on message length, enquirers are likely to think of them as short, punchy media, not really suitable for lengthy communications. Enquirers are very likely to be using them on small-screen devices, too, with all that that implies about message and sentence length.

Above all, though, the clue is in the name of such services: **instant messaging** or **chat**. These are real-time services, where people expect to have a conversation whose fluency is limited only by the time it takes for each party to type their response. So if you are using such media to respond to enquiries, don't expect to be able to simply send your answer and sign the enquiry off. Assume instead that your enquirer is likely to come back to you pretty quickly – possibly with a supplementary question and expecting a reasonably quick response.

Screen presentations

All these design considerations apply when you need to present answers on screen too. You're not restricted to headings and bullet points when you use presentation packages; you can treat the screen as a blank canvas onto which you can place text, images and objects wherever you like for maximum impact. Look, for example, at the way television presenters show complex information in simple visual form – using a composite image of appropriate elements as a background to a subject like the economy, science or social issues. Facts and figures will be displayed on an appropriate surface – a brick wall for a report on graffiti, a football pitch for a sports report. Again, all of these techniques are replicable using standard presentation software – and it's also worth bearing in mind that presentation software is an effective static design medium too, allowing you to create attractive visuals (such as infographics) that you can then drop into your final word processed report.

If your answer covers a complex topic that comes up over and over again, it might even be worth considering presenting it as a set of HTML pages, to be stored permanently on your corporate intranet and amended as required. Presenting information in this way enables you to provide plenty of structure and flexibility – breaking detail down into digestible chunks and using links and other navigation aids such as breadcrumbs to guide your enquirer around. If you do decide to go down this route, though, it's worth taking a look at the World Wide Web Consortium (W3C) Web Content Accessibility Guidelines. These offer masses of useful advice on things like: how to make your navigation consistent; effective use of section headings; optimum line width and spacing, and text size; colour contrast for improved readability; and how to make links self-evident and their use intuitive.

But is any of this worth the effort? That's up to you. It is certainly all too easy to get carried away and concentrate on the presentation to the detriment of the content. But bear in mind that such techniques are tried and tested in the media, and that decision-makers probably have to sit through lots and lots of boring presentations consisting of nothing but headings and bullet points. So if you can create one really compelling design template that you then can use over and over, it could be time well invested in terms of the impact your service makes on its clientele.

Enhancing answers on paper

And let's not forget the humble piece of paper. If you're supplying a photocopy for your enquirer to keep, or if you're faxing the information back, mark the crucial sections. Highlight the relevant paragraph with a marker pen. Put asterisks against the most useful entries in a directory or bibliography. Draw a line down the required column or across the required row of a table of statistics. Put in an arrow head to point out the key component of a diagram. Circle the right place on a map. And, whatever else you do, make sure that the source of your document is clearly cited. Underline it if it's already printed there; write it in if not. These are suggestions, of course, not hard-and-fast rules. But, as a general principle, do whatever you can to lead your enquirer to the information they want as rapidly and clearly as possible. The cost of doing such things is minuscule, the customer relations value immense.

Research reports

Finally, if you have to provide answers in the form of reports based on desk research then, in addition to all the other value you can add, you need to think about the look and feel of your documents too. Once again, this isn't an optional extra; it's a vital part of promoting your service, keeping it relevant in the eyes of decision-makers, and ensuring that it survives and thrives. In fact, it's so important that we're going to look at turning your search results into research reports in a lot more detail in Chapter 7.

Copyright, licensing, ethics

There are ethical considerations to bear in mind when manipulating text, numbers or images to enhance an answer. Be sure that you make it quite clear what you have done with the version of the document that you finally present to your enquirer, so that they are in no doubt as to how it varies from the original. (And, as always, make sure that you cite the source in full in your answer.)

Just as crucial are copyright and licensing. Put very simply, **copyright** (including database rights) provides statutory protection for authors, permitting them to exploit their intellectual property in any way they wish, and putting strict limits on what others may do with it, for a legally defined period; **licensing** is a contract agreement between the content supplier and purchaser, specifying in detail what the user may and may not do with that particular content. As a general rule, licences should extend what is permissible under copyright law, not further restrict it. Copyright and licensing can affect activities such as lending, copying, scanning, faxing, downloading – and enquiry answering.

Copyright law can vary widely from country to country – and there may sometimes be some leeway. Some jurisdictions may have **fair dealing** (or fair use) exemptions, permitting copying for research and private study, or for criticism, review, quotation or news reporting. Some governments have relaxed copyright restrictions on use of official publications. When it comes to licensing, **Creative Commons** (CC) licences allow creators of intellectual property to specify which rights they preserve and which they waive so that others can make use of their work. However, you'll need to bear in mind that there are a variety of different CC licences available; they don't all permit modification and not all permit commercial use either. Finally, **Royalty Free** licences can allow the user to use material – particularly images – in return for payment of a single fee, without the need to pay additionally for each use.

So before you engage in any value-added activity of this kind, be sure that you understand the terms on which the content concerned has been supplied to you. If the licence forbids supply of copies to a third party – for example, to enquirers who are not members of your college – then, no matter how much you may regret the missed opportunity, you must not do it. As a general principle, in fact, you should make sure that you understand all the copyright and licensing requirements under which your library or information service operates before you start any enquiry work. Copying in all media has now become so easy that publishers are understandably more and more vigilant about infringements – including doing things like marking the content as theirs by embedding a digital watermark into an image.

So the message is: copyright and licensing are a big deal. Nothing could be worse for your customer relations than promising something that the rules don't subsequently allow you to deliver. If you're in any doubt about what you're allowed to do, read them up or seek advice.

Has the answer arrived – and does the enquirer like it?

Yet again, when the enquirer is with you and you've been working on an enquiry together, it's relatively easy to tell when it's finally finished and whether the enquirer is satisfied with the answer. To put it bluntly, you ask them and they tell you. But, as we've seen so often already, it's all very different when the enquirer is somewhere else.

So first of all, has the answer actually arrived where it was supposed to? Not much doubt if it's something simple and brief which you phone through. But if the enquirer doesn't answer, you might have to leave a message with their colleague or on their voicemail, asking them to call you back. And do you risk actually leaving the answer in a voicemail message? It may be confidential and something that the enquirer doesn't want to risk others in their organization finding out. Of course, if you've done your job properly (see Chapter 2), you'll have at least two means of contacting them. But whatever the outcome, it's likely to mean a delay before you can finally sign off the enquiry.

And if you're replying using a text-based medium – e-mail, text, instant messaging – you have little guarantee that the enquiry has arrived safely, and none at all that the enquirer is satisfied. Asking for a 'Delivery' or a 'Read' receipt for an e-mail tells you nothing either; it simply means that someone, somewhere, opened it. It doesn't tell you if it's the right person, and certainly not whether it's what they wanted. So if you don't hear back from the enquirer with an acknowledgement pretty soon, contact them again to check – possibly using the same medium as you did before but preferably using a different one. Phone if you originally e-mailed; leave a text on their mobile if you got no response from their landline. If this all seems terribly tedious – a bit 'belt and braces' – remember that it's better than having a discontented customer on your hands. They might never tell you about their discontent, so you'll never be able to take remedial action. But they may well tell lots of their friends, potentially damaging your reputation in the process.

Sign-off: what can we learn from this enquiry?

With the enquirer satisfied and the enquiry signed off your task is nearly over. But before you finally file it away, there's still one more piece of value you can add – value to your own organization. If the enquiry was anything other than routine, there are some really useful lessons to be learned from it – plus quite possibly new information sources to consider and new services that you could introduce as a result.

So take some time to review the completed enquiry. Assess it for its difficulty and the time it took. Look carefully at the sources and delivery media you used; there are likely to be some new ones, and you need to consider whether or not it might be worth purchasing or subscribing to them. You may possibly have contacted some useful new organizations as well; you'll need to decide how to record them so you can benefit from their expertise again in the future. The enquiry may even have suggested to you an entirely new service that you could offer as a result, in which case you will have a lot of thinking to do, deciding how best to introduce and manage it. Completing an enquiry successfully isn't the end; it's the start of the next phase in your enquiry service. So let's look at some of these considerations in more detail . . .

How successful were you?

Just as we said in Chapter 1 that you mustn't accept a vague deadline, so you shouldn't tolerate an imprecise measure of success either. It's all too easy for a complacent colleague to record as 'successful' an enquiry that a more conscientious one might regard as only partially successful. Taken to its extreme, this could result in the more conscientious one ending up with a poorer annual appraisal report than the complacent one (and even a lower salary increase), simply because they were more honest and realistic in recording their degree of success.

So instead, you should go for more objective measures. If you've been meticulous in agreeing with the enquirer precisely what you were going to do for them, and had worked out exactly what the final answer would look like, then it should be possible to apply one of three measures of success – complete, partial or compromise.

Complete success means that you have provided an answer that met the enquirer's needs in every respect. In the school governors query, for example, this would mean that you had: discovered how the Strong & Moral Britain Association was funded and whether or not it was associated with neo-fascist organizations; been able to provide some authoritative guidelines on what obligations school governors faced regarding declaration of other interests; and found details of what the enquirer's brother had been saying about immigrants in council. Anything much less than this, and you would probably have to record the degree of success as 'partial'.

Partial success means that you have been able to find some of what the enquirer wants, but not all. You may, for example, have come up with some figures on migration patterns in Wales which showed general trends over a period for the whole country, but not necessarily the degree of detail that the enquirer would have liked – nothing on specific movements into and out of Glamorgan, for example. In this case, you've certainly provided an answer that will get the enquirer started, but not enough to enable them to finish their task to their satisfaction; so you've probably referred them somewhere else as well. (We'll deal with recording referrals in a moment.)

Compromise means that you and the enquirer have together agreed on an answer that was not exactly what they originally wanted, but which is an acceptable alternative nevertheless. In the Westminster Aquarium query, you may have agreed to supplement the paltry and repetitive offerings you can provide on the Aquarium itself with background on Victorian entertainments, or rival attractions of the period, just to enable the enquirer to complete the project to their supervisor's satisfaction. This is not an ideal outcome, and you must of course have agreed it with the enquirer. But it's about as close to an admission of failure as you should ever allow your enquiry service to come.

Should you ever need to record that you were completely unsuccessful? Hopefully not. Remember the promise you gave when you were starting to think about how you would answer the enquiry back in Chapter 3? 'I'm sure I can help' was what you said – and so you can, even if you and the enquirer eventually had to compromise on what kind of answer would be acceptable. If you ever felt that you had to record a result as 'unsuccessful', that would probably just mean that the enquiry wasn't finished yet. (Note, too, that we haven't talked about referrals; we'll come back to those in a moment.)

Was the enquirer satisfied?

As well as recording your success objectively, you should also seek as objective a measure as possible of the enquirer's satisfaction with the result. You could collect survey data for the purpose either locally using for example a simple spreadsheet, or online using proprietary survey software with its associated analytics capabilities.

To measure satisfaction you could invite the enquirer to choose between the same words as you used to measure your success – Complete, Partial, Compromise. That would give a direct comparison between your and the enquirer's perceptions of success, which could provide valuable management data showing how your service is regarded and perhaps revealing patterns indicating where you might need improvements.

Or you could ask the enquirer a question like: 'On a scale of 1 to 5, how satisfied were you with the answer you received (1 being dissatisfied and 5 being completely satisfied)?' If you use this method, you (or your management) will need to think carefully about what range of scores to offer. A scale of 1 to 10 could give you useful percentage scores, but it's a very long scale for your enquirer to get their head round. But if you use 1 to 5, that allows the enquirer to sit on the fence by choosing 3. Using 1 to 4 would enable you to analyse satisfaction by quartiles – but it's so close to the 3 to 1 scale implicit in the 'Complete, Partial, Compromise' measure that you might as well use that instead. So no answers here – just some food for thought.

While your measure of success is hopefully as objective as possible, your enquirer's perception could be a great deal more subjective. You'll encounter some enquirers who are effusively appreciative of answers that actually took you very little time to find, while others may be distinctly unimpressed no matter how much effort you've had to go to. The moral from this is that you shouldn't rely on too little enquirer satisfaction data; only a large dataset can begin to reduce the subjectivity of individual enquirer responses.

How long did it take to answer?

In recording this, you'll need to consider whether the time it took was pretty much what you would have expected, or whether it took longer. If it did take longer, was this because it was more difficult than you expected, or just more time-consuming? These are not necessarily the same thing, and it comes back to the easy/hard quick/slow decisions you had to take when you were deciding on the working timetable for prioritizing your enquiries (Chapter 5). It is vitally important to know how long enquiries take to answer, because time is money. If there's a pattern to the difficult and/or lengthy enquiries then that raises implications about the appropriateness and value of the sources and delivery media you're using. Perhaps you need to invest in something new – and maybe you'll be able to offer some useful new services as a result. (We'll come back to this a little later on.)

Did you meet the deadline?

There are only two possible answers to this – yes or no. Nothing else will do, and if you're recording 'No' a lot in this box then, again, you need to do some serious thinking about why, and what you can do to improve your 'Yes' score. If you had to negotiate more time (you didn't just present a late answer without warning the enquirer that that was going to happen, did you?) then you need to record your reasons – not just to get you off the hook but so you can decide what service improvements are needed to try to prevent it happening again. It may well be that the enquiry took a long time because you just didn't know what would be the best sources or delivery media to get you started. Well, now you do. So record them, and make use of what you have learned the next time a similar enquiry comes up. (We'll come back to this too in a moment.)

Did you have to refer the enquiry elsewhere?

If you recorded partial success or a compromise outcome, then that may well mean that you also referred the enquiry to another organization. This should trigger a whole range of questions about how your service might be able to change and develop as a result. If it's an organization that you have never used before then, first, how did you discover it? If it was through a directory (print or electronic) then does that mean that that directory is actually more useful than you previously thought it was? Have you checked the new organization's website to find out what else it can offer? Is that site worth bookmarking as a Favourite for future reference? If so, where is the best place to put it in your bookmarks classification?

And what about the organization itself? When you contacted it (You did contact it, didn't you? You didn't just leave the enquirer to make a cold call?) were the staff both helpful and useful (not necessarily the same thing)? If they were both helpful and useful, did they help out of goodwill? Or does the organization have an agenda to pursue? If the former, then you should certainly be grateful, but shouldn't necessarily rely on that goodwill persisting if you keep going back to it time and time again. At some point, you may need to decide what kind of long-term relationship you want to have with it (see below). If it has an agenda, then that's fine just as long as you're clear what that agenda is. If you went looking for expert help on the health effects of radiation, for example, you may get exactly the same information from both Public Health England (a government body) and Friends of the Earth (an environmental pressure group) – but they might put different interpretations on that information. Or if you contact an industry or trade organization, you'll need to know whether it's on the producer or consumer side of the fence, or whether it represents employers or employees – something which may not necessarily be obvious from its name.

Melodramatic as it may seem, you'll also need to know whether the organizations you contact are discreet. If an enquirer approaches an organization on your advice, and subsequently finds themselves bombarded with unsolicited communications from it, then they're likely to be upset with you at the intrusion on their privacy and, quite possibly, the infringement of data protection as well. And if your approach to the organization or – even worse – your enquirer's approach becomes public without your or their consent, then you're in even bigger trouble. You may, of course, have redress against the organization under data protection law, but by that time the damage will have been done. So the moral is: ask immediately whether the organization handles all enquiries in confidence. This still doesn't guarantee that it really will do so, of course – but at least you have it on record that you did ask and that it gave you an assurance.

Assuming that your referral organization has passed all these tests, you'll finally need to consider your long-term relationship with it. It may be a trade association or professional body that offers a charged-for enquiry or advice service, which you might consider subscribing to. This is a big decision, of course, with implications for your budget, so it's not to be undertaken lightly. But you can't undertake it at all unless you have recorded the enquiry properly in the first place.

Did you discover any useful new resources?

Sometimes a source you already subscribe to but have never really had the time to get to know properly will turn out to be ideal for a particular kind of enquiry that has always foxed you in the past. So when you do discover a useful new source – whether print or electronic – make sure you have procedures in place for recording it properly. The form those take will depend on the nature of the searching aids you have already chosen to develop for your service. You may be exploiting your library management system to do this, customizing its discovery tools for the purpose. Or you may have your own Know-How or Frequently Asked Questions (FAQs) file that you post to your organization's intranet. Instantly updatable at any time, this should also enable you to create automatic links to any websites or e-mail addresses or centrally stored electronic documents that you include in it.

If it's on your intranet, everybody in the organization can have access to it. If it's just a file on your network drive, then you'll probably need to make it read-only, so that only authorized people can make changes after due consideration and so your indexing remains up to standard. However, you could consider using a social tool – perhaps one already available through your integrated library system – thereby allowing other people in the organization to add their own comments. An intranet-based FAQ or Know-How file, reflecting your resources and services and including live links to internal sources of information or expertise, could in fact turn out to be one of the most valuable resources you could provide.

When you discover a new source that you don't currently have at all, then you need to consider whether it's worth purchasing or subscribing to. If you decide that it is, you should also consider which delivery medium would be most useful for you. (Sometimes content vendors insist on a combined print and online package, even if one of these two would have been sufficient on its own.) You'll also need to examine any copyright or licensing requirements, to ensure that you are entitled to exploit it in the way you want. If, for example, you intend to network the new source direct to your users throughout the organization, then there are likely to be cost implications, because licence fees often vary depending on how many desks you intend to serve. (See above for a bit more on copyright and licensing.)

Finally, you should have procedures in place for telling both your colleagues and your users about new services that you can offer as a result of new sources acquired. And remember, too, that it should be that way round. Your enquirers aren't interested in sources, but in outcomes. You could use something as simple as a regularly e-mailed current awareness bulletin or newsletter – but even better would be to put these details on your corporate intranet, perhaps using software that supports collaborative working and allows users to comment on how useful they have found specific sources to be.

Developing and maintaining services like these can all take time that you may feel you can ill afford when there are other pressing enquiries to be answered. But do try to make time to investigate new sources and to ensure you are fully exploiting the ones you already have. It will pay enormous dividends, and will mean that you will be able to provide an even better enquiry service in the future.

Coming next – adding even more value

We've been performing literature searches and delivering the results to our enquirers since the beginning of time. But now – in fields like government, regulation, business, law, health – enquirers are demanding more. They are busy people, and simply don't have time to wade through the unstructured search results for themselves. They are increasingly expecting us information professionals to bring some order to the content we retrieve on their behalf. So how can you turn your raw search results into a polished, value-added summary of the findings, in the minimum amount of time and with maximum efficiency? This matters not just for those who actually carry out desk research on their clients' behalf, but also for those whose job is to encourage good research practice in others, such as students doing assignments. So in the next chapter, we're going to think about adding even more value – by synthesizing search results into a narrative research report or student assignment. And to do this efficiently yet quickly, we need to exercise our critical thinking skills.

To recap . . .

- **Quality-check your answer before you deliver it.**
- **Plan your oral or written presentation carefully.**
- **Make sure you observe copyright and licensing requirements.**
- **Use completed enquiries to improve your success rate and develop your service.**
- **Apply your creative thinking skills to ensuring your service inspires confidence.**

CHAPTER 7

Don't just give me another reading list!

Using critical thinking skills to add further value to your answer

In this chapter you'll find out how to:

- **manipulate, categorize and prioritize your search results**
- **identify the essential information your enquirer needs**
- **read key documents strategically instead of sequentially**
- **summarize your search results in report form**
- **use critical thinking for quick decisions on what's worth using and what's not.**

Spotlight is a movie that tells the true story of how journalists at the *Boston Globe* lifted the lid on a major cover-up in the Roman Catholic Church. During their investigations, the team did everything you would expect investigative journalists to do: they door-stepped people; they confronted leading figures; they waited for hours in outer offices trying to grab interviews. But the backbone of their research was a simple spreadsheet onto which they made entries from back issues of the *Massachusetts Catholic Directory*. It was this that enabled them to spot the suspicious patterns of behaviour that underpinned their revelations.

This kind of activity is increasing dramatically in importance. At the rocket science end of the spectrum, it's manifesting itself as Big Data, where analysts develop and employ applications to trawl vast quantities of data, looking for patterns that can be turned into e-commerce or other opportunities. But the principle of applying critical analysis to retrieved data operates across the board – including to the human brain power that we bring to bear in carrying out literature searches.

Of course, we mere mortals do face limitations – mainly in the tiny amount of content we are capable of evaluating within a sensible timescale compared with what computers can achieve. But that doesn't mean that we're incapable of doing it. We've already looked briefly at some of the principles of good time management in Chapter 5 and, crucially, at the distinction between vital and urgent tasks. And it's with this next task in particular – synthesizing your search results into a narrative report on the findings – that those principles really demonstrate their value.

Techniques such as those described in this chapter carry obvious lessons for information professionals who carry out desk research on their users' behalf. But they're no less valuable for academic librarians too. Charged with promoting and encouraging good information literacy practice, they can draw their own users' attention to the benefits such techniques can offer and the higher quality of research they are likely to produce as a result. So, as with the searching techniques we looked at in Chapter 4, information professionals whose job is to encourage good research practice in others, such as students doing assignments, should find masses in this chapter that they can also pass on to those they support – in particular, use of critical thinking skills.

POWER and KISS

Underlying this process of adding value to your raw search results – the unstructured mass of documents you (or your students) initially retrieve – are two principles: POWER and KISS. POWER is a handy acronym for the process you need to go through – Plan, Organize, Write, Edit, Review – and KISS helps you remember the underlying rule in this and, indeed, pretty much all your work: Keep It Simple, Stupid! Let's begin by unpacking these two acronyms and seeing how they can assist.

Plan

This is where you map out the whole process, from downloading the raw search results to delivering the narrative summary to your enquirer. As we saw in Chapter 5, it's a time management process; you need to provisionally allocate time to the key stages – organizing the retrieved results, writing them up, editing them into a coherent narrative and finally reviewing the effectiveness of the answer you eventually delivered to your enquirer. Of course, at this stage, the time allocations are necessarily provisional; you don't yet know what unexpected problems you're going to face. But if you approach the task systematically you should be able to start spotting what's really important right from the start, and adjust your schedule accordingly.

We've already looked at the issues that need to concern us when doing the actual searching, in Chapter 4. So let's assume that we've completed that stage – or helped our enquirer to do so – and that we now have a set of raw search results, which may have come from a multitude of sources and be in a whole range of different formats.

Organize

Wading through search results like these can waste an awful lot of your time if you're not careful. You can't really do anything with them until you've brought order to this confusion by categorizing the documents retrieved. Within the broad subject specified by your enquirer ('Migration patterns in Wales' for example) you'll probably need to sort the documents into topics – distinguishing between those that cover the social or economic effects of migration, for instance, or separating the commentary out from the raw statistical data.

You'll also probably want to be able to arrange your documents quickly and easily by date of publication, so you can see which ones are likely to have influenced which others. You might want to distinguish them according to their source – separating government policy documents from academic studies, for example. And – a tricky one this – you'll undoubtedly need to take a view on which are the most authoritative documents, the ones most likely to be useful to your enquirer.

Classifying your retrieved documents in this way will help you decide: which ones you are likely to feature in your narrative summary; which you might simply refer to briefly; and whether there are any that, on reflection, can be ignored altogether. This is the stage that will almost certainly take the most time – longer than actually writing the summary – but it will be time well invested nevertheless. And you can still take steps to minimize the amount of work you need to do on this stage; we'll return to that in a moment.

Write

You might think that actually writing up the search results is going to be the most time-consuming stage – but you'd probably be wrong! If you have organized your results effectively then the writing can be pretty straightforward; in many cases, you may well be able to lift content directly from the abstracts of your chosen documents, in a logical order, to create your first draft. Of course you still need to tell a good story to your enquirer; again, we'll come back to that later on.

Edit

Once you've got your draft down you'll then need to polish it, so the disjointed sentences and phrases that you may have lifted from a whole range of different documents flow together smoothly to create a readable text. This is also the stage at which you (or a colleague) need to look carefully for any errors, ambiguities or potentially misleading statements.

Review

This stage comes after you have delivered your answer. First of all you need enquirer feedback – especially if they're not satisfied (something that we looked at in Chapter 6). Second, this is your opportunity to reflect on the entire process to see if you can streamline it and make it more time-efficient in the future. In other words, Keep It Simple, Stupid . . .

KISS

Going through all these stages may seem like an awful lot of work. But you don't have to complete every POWER stage right down to the last detail. As we saw when it came to quality-checking your answer, in Chapter 6, you just need to do enough to allow your enquirer to take a decision, make a recommendation or take action. This applies particularly to the Organize stage – you just need to do it well enough to be able to move on. You may decide, for example, that the search subject is so specific that you don't need to categorize the documents by topic – or that so few of them are really useful that you can focus instead on the handful that are and ignore the rest.

And if the KISS principle works for information professionals who do their own desk research, then it works even more for those who are trying to encourage good research practice in others. Students famously don't leave themselves enough time for anything; there are always more interesting things going on elsewhere in their lives. If you can demonstrate to them that techniques such as these not only save them time in the long run but also enable them to complete their assignments more efficiently – that's a win-win situation that will benefit them for the rest of their lives.

Those are all the stages you need to consider when you **Plan** how to add value to your search results. Let's see how it works in practice from here on . . .

Making your search results manipulable

Remember in Chapter 1 we had an enquirer asking about migration patterns in Wales? Having quickly established that the subject was people in the principality, not sea mammals, we then asked a series of questions to try to firm up on the search parameters. What kinds of movement? Just current patterns or back over a period? Just the raw figures or comment on them as well? From all of this, we should have been able to agree with the enquirer a detailed brief for the search – something like . . .

What has the scale of migration in Wales been over the last decade? How has it affected the ethnic mix in Wales? What social and economic impact has that had on the population of Wales?

Now it's starting to look like a classic student assignment – in which case part of your job would be to advise your enquirer on possible sources to use (try some of the Starter Sources mentioned in Chapter 8 on Choosing Your Toolkit, perhaps). You'd also probably want to help them frame a successful search strategy – to understand, for example, that they would need to corral separately the different concepts: what kinds of people are migrating (Who); the activities they're engaging in (What); their countries of origin or destination (Where). They'll also need to be aware of other terms related to words like 'social' ('housing', 'community') and 'economic' ('employment', 'business'). And they'll need to understand that 'impact' is not a good word to include in the search strategy because it is a soft term with many synonyms – 'effects', 'consequences', 'outcomes'. (See Chapter 4 for a recap on all of this.)

Exactly the same considerations apply if you have to do the search yourself, of course – and with such a potentially wide-ranging subject as this, you're likely to end up with a lot of retrieved documents. Remember when we talked about imagining the final answer in Chapter 3? Well, the possibilities with a subject like this are endless: figures, obviously – which may also be expressed as graphs, charts or maps; but also text – from official reports, academic studies, textbooks, journalism, diaries, blogs; and lists – countries of origin or destination, nationalities, languages, skills.

Anyway, let's assume that you've done a viable search (or your student has), during which you may have had to visit several different repositories of content to retrieve all the documents you need. The job now is to find a way of making sense of them all, with maximum efficiency and minimum expenditure of time – and the way they are now, that's not going to be easy. Take a look, for example, at these few results.

Document	Type	Topic
A critical reflection on the research priorities for improving the health and social care to black and minority ethnic groups in Wales	Academic study	Social
Migrant entrepreneurship and ethnic community development: Polish small businesses in Cardiff, Wales	Article	Economic
Migrant crisis: how Wales will respond	Broadcast news item	Political
Immigration and inclusion in South Wales	Report	Social
COMPAS: Migration services in Wales	Research project website	Social
Statistics on migrant workers in Wales	Statistics	Economic
Italians in Wales and their cultural representations, 1920s–2010s	Textbook	Cultural
Shelter investigates hidden story of homelessness in Wales	Written news item	Social

This is just a tiny random sample of everything you've managed to retrieve; a search like this could easily retrieve at least 50–100 viable items, or even more – including speeches, lectures, visual presentations, blog postings, other social media comment, video clips – and that's by no means an exhaustive list. Because the documents could be in all sorts of different formats, reference management software may find it difficult to handle them all. (See Chapter 8 on Choosing Your Toolkit for examples of applications you could consider using.) The search results may also by now all be in one long downloaded list, so won't be easy to sort (beyond, possibly, their basic bibliographic characteristics). And, since you're likely to be looking at them on screen, you'll only be able to see a very small sample of the search results at any one time, and will need to rely on your short-term memory plus a lot of note-taking to start picking out the most promising ones. All in all, you risk wasting a lot of time trying to bring some order to the chaos you (or your student) may have retrieved. There has to be a better way to **Organize** them, and there is.

Creating a flexible dataset

What we need is a system to enable us to identify the most important documents within each type and – crucially – to be able to change our mind if we come across later documents that are more useful than the ones we've reviewed already. And we may need to sort and re-sort this list over and over again until we're satisfied that the best documents for our enquirer's purposes are coming to the top. Let's just think of some of the ways in which we might want to sort our retrieved documents . . .

Date: Organizing our documents by date could be useful, if we assume that the content of later documents is informed by earlier ones. However, date is a rather crude indicator of a document's usefulness.

Categories: Where we have retrieved a large number of documents, we're certainly going to need to arrange them into different categories, just to be able to make sense of them all. We may need subject categories, or categories indicating a document's status or authority or authorship, or all of these. (We're also going to need to think carefully about the names we give the various categories; if we don't keep the naming consistent we won't be able to sort them properly.)

Usefulness: We're definitely going to need to assess each document's usefulness in helping to answer the enquiry. Doing this will, for example, enable a student to decide which documents they will feature in their assignment report, and bring those to the head of the list in the right order when required. And exactly the same consideration applies if we've been commissioned to do the search ourselves and report back to the enquirer. If we can quickly prioritize our documents to determine the best ones for the job – and change our mind easily in the light of later findings – then the actual writing of the assignment or research report or literature review should become straightforward and quite quick.

Other characteristics: There are of course other details that we're going to need to capture – author, title and citation, for instance. There may be occasions when we briefly want to bring together all the documents by the same author – for example to distinguish between a substantive study and the various articles by the same author that may have been spun off it. And we may need to sort temporarily by title, for deduplication purposes. At some stage, too, it's going to be handy to capture – for the most useful documents at any rate – text that acts as a surrogate of the full content: an abstract, executive summary or set of findings for instance. (We'll come back to this later when we think about how to tell our story to our enquirer.)

The matrix

Remember those *Boston Globe* journalists? They made sense of all the information they were finding by dropping it into a spreadsheet – a matrix (or table or framework or grid) that allowed them to analyse the results. As soon as they did that, the patterns they were seeking became instantly apparent – something that probably wouldn't have happened if they'd just tried to work from their interviews and the entries in the original publication. And they were just using back issues of one source: the *Massachusetts Catholic Directory*. Just imagine how much more complex the task would have been if they'd had to wade through multiple sources in widely varying formats.

So it is with our Welsh migration query. To identify and manipulate the documents we've retrieved, we'll need to change the presentation of our search results from a linear list into a flexible dataset. Basically, we'll require a matrix into which we can insert the different types of information about each document – one row for each document and one column for each type of information.

To do this, you might be able to make use of your chosen reference management package. This should at least save you time by automating the presentation of each document's bibliographic characteristics, and you may then be able to add extra customized fields for the further ways in which you want to arrange your search results. You may also find that you have to add 'grey' literature – short reports, articles from non-mainstream sources, website content, ephemera – manually. Obviously making these manual additions could be time-consuming, but it will probably be time well invested because, once entered, the reference management software will treat these non-standard documents just the same as the others – ensuring a uniform format for every document and allowing you to create bibliographies automatically. So if you can use a reference management package to automate at least part of the process, that should save you a great deal of time at the next stage.

If you don't use reference management software, you could use any program that will support this kind of matrix structure – a spreadsheet or database package, the table function in a word-processed document, or any proprietary software that can be used for project management purposes. You may also be able to automate some of the process by making use of the text-to-table conversion function that comes with your word-processing package – although the resulting table may need so much repair that you may be no better off than if you had done the whole thing manually in the first place.

Obviously, the more you can automate the better – but whatever means you decide to use to restructure your search results, you will need to satisfy yourself that your chosen approach will enable you to:

- work with documents taken from any source you choose, not just mainstream ones
- describe those documents using whatever headings you want
- sort and re-sort the documents using multiple criteria determined by you.

If your scope for automating the process is minimal, and you find you do have to do the copying across to your matrix manually, then there's no getting away from the fact that it's going to be a pretty labour-intensive and tedious job. The KISS principle certainly applies here; you just copy across the minimum detail you need to enable you to start manipulating your findings in a meaningful way. But however you need to create your matrix, you might end up with a framework looking something like this (with as many rows as you're going to need to accommodate information on all your retrieved documents) . . .

Priority	Topic	Type	Title	Author	Citation	Date	Summary & Notes

So is it really going to be worth all the effort? That depends on the nature of the documents your search has retrieved. If you've only found a dozen or so, and it's obvious which ones are the best for your enquirer's purposes, then of course you don't need to go through all this tedious procedure. But if you've retrieved, say, 50 documents or more, and it's not immediately obvious which are the most useful ones, then going through this process will almost certainly represent a good investment of your time. It may actually save you time in the long run; but just as likely, you may end up using the same amount of time as you would trying to work from the original list of references, but using that time far more efficiently and cost-effectively.

It's worth pointing out, too, that you don't have to fill in every cell in every column you're currently populating – just the ones you need for immediate purposes. (Remember the KISS principle.) So, again looking for the moment at that same small sample of the documents retrieved, you may end up with a result looking something like the one shown immediately below. (NB In each of the examples shown throughout the rest of this chapter, I've compressed some of the columns so you can see clearly the ones that matter at each stage; obviously this wouldn't be necessary when you were doing this for real.)

***	***	***	Title	Author	Citation	Date	Summary & Notes
			A critical reflection on the research priorities for improving the health and social care to black and minority ethnic groups in Wales	Charlotte Williams, Keele University Joy Merrell, Swansea University et al.	*Diversity in Health and Social Care 2007;* 4:193–9	20070000	
			Migrant entrepreneurship and ethnic community development: Polish small businesses in Cardiff, Wales	Julie Porter	*International Journal of Interdisciplinary Social Sciences* **4**(1) pp355–368	20090000	
			Migrant crisis: how Wales will respond	The Wave	The Wave 96.4 FM	20150917	Web report from radio station
			Immigration and inclusion in South Wales	Joseph Rowntree Foundation		20080810	
			COMPAS: Migration services in Wales	Centre on Migration, Policy, and Society (COMPAS)			Research project website, accessed 160713
			Statistics on migrant workers in Wales	Statistics for Wales		20090827	
			Italians in Wales and their cultural representations, 1920s–2010s	Bruna Chezzi	Cambridge Scholars	20150000	
			Shelter investigates hidden story of homelessness in Wales	Big Lottery Fund Shelter Cymru		20081212	

Sorting your documents by date

We've already looked at the possibility that you might sometimes want to sort your documents by date, and deciding how to manage that is worth a little bit of consideration too. We've seen in Chapter 4 the importance when searching of distinguishing between the American way of citing dates and that used in most of the rest of the world. But dates can come in all sorts of other formats as well: March 14th 1989; 14 March '89; 14/3/1989; 03.14.89.

It may be that the package you've decided to use is pretty clever at distinguishing dates in different formats and you can rely on it getting it right automatically – but if you're at all unsure, you can opt instead for an unambiguous numeric representation of a date: 19890314 in this instance. That's what we've done in the example shown above, and this convention will also work when no day is specified; you simply turn something like 'March '89' into 19890300 if you want documents dated this way to come out at the top of your list, or 19890399 if you want them at the bottom.

Selecting, rejecting, prioritizing

Now you can really start adding value to what you've retrieved – by assigning categories to each document and – crucially – deciding which ones are going to be the most useful from your enquirer's point of view. So . . .

Classifying your documents by topic or type . . .

Hopefully you won't have allowed yourself to go into a mindless state if you've had to do manual copying across. You'll have been thinking briefly about each document record as you handle it, and starting to form a view as to how you might want to categorize it. Some documents may subdivide the main subject of the search into smaller topics – in which case you may need a column in your matrix headed 'Topic'. You may also decide at this stage that it wouldn't be helpful to sort these topics alphabetically, so you might want to add a letter or number to each topic to reflect the order in which you want them to appear in the matrix.

Within those topics, some items could be major policy documents, some academic studies, others may provide good practice guidelines, and others again may be case studies showing how the guidelines have been put into operation – in which case you might need to create an extra column headed, for example, 'Type'. The way you decide to classify your retrieved documents will vary from one search to the next, and will largely be dictated by the enquirer's requirements. But the fundamental structure of the matrix, and the principles that lie behind it, remain the same with any complex set of search results, regardless of the subject of the enquiry.

So – looking again at our small sample of retrieved documents – you may by now have been able to add Topics and Types . . .

Priority	Topic	Type	Title	Author	***	***	***
	B: Social	Article	A critical reflection on the research priorities for improving the health and social care to black and minority ethnic groups in Wales	Charlotte Williams, Keele University Joy Merrell, Swansea University et al.			
	D: Ethnic groups	Article	Migrant entrepreneurship and ethnic community development: Polish small businesses in Cardiff, Wales	Julie Porter			
	B: Social	News	Migrant crisis: how Wales will respond	The Wave			
	B: Social	Report	*Immigration and inclusion in South Wales*	Joseph Rowntree Foundation			
	B: Social	Information	COMPAS: Migration services in Wales	Centre on Migration, Policy, and Society (COMPAS)			
	C: Economic	Statistics	Statistics on migrant workers in Wales	Statistics for Wales			
	D: Ethnic groups	Book	*Italians in Wales and their cultural representations, 1920s–2010s*	Bruna Chezzi			
	B: Social	News	Shelter investigates hidden story of homelessness in Wales	Big Lottery Fund Shelter Cymru			

Next – classifying them by how useful they are . . .

By this stage, some documents may already have struck you as being particularly useful or important from the enquirer's point of view. Now that their brief details are sitting in your matrix, you can assign a level of priority to each document and then sort the results to ensure that the most important ones rise to the top. But first, we need a rigorous system for ranking those documents, and there's a useful one that you might like to apply now: Must Know, Should Know and Could Know. This is how it works . . .

Must Know documents are the handful of retrieved results that are so comprehensive and so authoritative that you're going to use them as the basis for your report (or your student as the basis of their assignment). 'Must Know' information is the kind you would impart if you were doing a three-minute elevator pitch; it's absolutely crucial to the understanding of the issue and its importance, and it also persuades the listener (or reader) that they need to take the totality of the information seriously.

Should Know documents are the ones that provide essential supporting information in more detail than you can include in your elevator pitch. They might provide evidence supporting the main findings, or include case studies demonstrating how the techniques outlined in the Must Know documents would work in practice.

Could Know documents include the rest of your viable results. They might provide some additional detail that could be helpful if the enquirer really wanted to review the available literature comprehensively. They might include commentary on the more authoritative documents or simply be articles summarizing the originals. Either way, they're not going to add a great deal more to your enquirer's understanding of the subject.

In addition, you may have retrieved other documents which on consideration turn out to be irrelevant – perhaps because they're false hits, containing some of the search terms but not in the sense or context required. Do you have a usefulness classification for these? Of course not! You don't need to transfer them to your matrix at all – remember the KISS rule.

Finally, we have to remember that we need a classification of usefulness that we can sort on easily. Just using the words 'Must', 'Should' and 'Could' won't do; the only way we can sort these is alphabetically A–Z or Z–A, neither of which gives you a useful order of priority. Far better to use a numerical value, ranging from 1 (Must Know) to 3 (Could Know). That makes the classification unambiguous and gives you a self-evident result when you sort. Applying principles such as these, you could end up with something like . . .

Priority	Topic	Type	Title	Author	***	***	***
2	B: Social	Article	A critical reflection on the research priorities for improving the health and social care to black and minority ethnic groups in Wales	Charlotte Williams, Keele University Joy Merrell, Swansea University et al.			
2	D: Ethnic groups	Article	Migrant entrepreneurship and ethnic community development: Polish small businesses in Cardiff, Wales	Julie Porter			
3	B: Social	News	Migrant crisis: how Wales will respond	The Wave			
1	B: Social	Report	*Immigration and inclusion in South Wales*	Joseph Rowntree Foundation			
3	B: Social	Information	COMPAS: Migration services in Wales	Centre on Migration, Policy, and Society (COMPAS)			
1	C: Economic	Statistics	Statistics on migrant workers in Wales	Statistics for Wales			
3	D: Ethnic groups	Book	*Italians in Wales and their cultural representations, 1920s–2010s*	Bruna Chezzi			
2	B: Social	News	Shelter investigates hidden story of homelessness in Wales	Big Lottery Fund Shelter Cymru			

Finally organizing your search results – the real value-add

We've now made all the decisions we need to, and populated the cells in our matrix accordingly. But they're not yet in the order we want them. We'll probably want to sort them by priority first, within that by topic, and then possibly finally by date. But, pretty much whichever package you use, that final sorting stage should just be a couple of clicks – the work of a moment. So, still working for now with our small demonstration sample – you'll end up with this . . .

Priority	Topic	Type	Title	Author	***	***	***
1	B: Social	Report	*Immigration and inclusion in South Wales*	Joseph Rowntree Foundation			
1	C: Economic	Statistics	Statistics on migrant workers in Wales	Statistics for Wales			
2	B: Social	News	Shelter investigates hidden story of homelessness in Wales	Big Lottery Fund Shelter Cymru			
2	B: Social	Article	A critical reflection on the research priorities for improving the health and social care to black and minority ethnic groups in Wales	Charlotte Williams, Keele University Joy Merrell, Swansea University et al.			
2	D: Ethnic groups	Article	Migrant entrepreneurship and ethnic community development: Polish small businesses in Cardiff, Wales	Julie Porter			
3	B: Social	News	Migrant crisis: how Wales will respond	The Wave			
3	B: Social	Information	COMPAS: Migration services in Wales	Centre on Migration, Policy, and Society (COMPAS)			
3	D: Ethnic groups	Book	*Italians in Wales and their cultural representations, 1920s–2010s*	Bruna Chezzi			

You don't have to agree with the priorities I've assigned here, of course; they're just to demonstrate the principle. The crucial point, though, is that at this stage (as with the *Boston Globe* spreadsheet) the patterns become clear – and they may induce you to change some of the priorities or other classifications. You may decide that a document to which you assigned a lower priority now requires a higher one, or that a document you thought looked particularly promising when you were reviewing each one individually doesn't look so good now that you can see it alongside other similar ones. If so, it's the work of a moment to change its priority score and re-sort – as many times as you need to.

If you do only this much, you've already added an enormous amount of value to your initial unsorted trawl of miscellaneous documents. If you're an information professional supporting researchers or practitioners, you can save them valuable time and effort by simply handing over the matrix and inviting them to pick the documents they want to see (or providing direct links in the matrix itself if you can). And if your job is to encourage good research practice in students, then introducing them to procedures such as this can constitute one of the best services you could render. Remember when you were a student, and your tutors dinned into you the need to plan the structure of your essay, dissertation or assignment report before writing anything (not to mention providing a good bibliography at the end)? Techniques such as this can enable your students to do just that, and make more efficient use of their limited time as well.

But if you want to take it a stage further there's even more value you can add – by using your matrix as the basis for a narrative report. Whether it's a student being supported by you, or desk research that you're expected to undertake yourself, you or your student are now much closer than you may think to being able to write your research up – systematically, coherently and confidently. But before we move onto the business of finally writing up the results, let's divert for a moment and explore the fascinating practice of strategic reading.

Strategic reading – finding the best bits of each document

As we discussed briefly in Chapter 4, there's sometimes no alternative to dipping into the text of the original document to discover what it's about – and it's at this stage in the process of turning your raw search results into an actionable report that these techniques really come into their own. You may need to deploy them yourself, if you're working directly to an enquirer – or you might alternatively want to recommend them to the students or researchers who you're supporting. Students, in particular, always have masses of reading and probably rarely feel they have enough time to do it; introduce them to some of these time-saving techniques for getting through their reading and you'll have done them a service that will benefit them for the rest of their lives.

Where to sample

We saw in Chapter 4 that the trick is knowing what not to read – going immediately to the best bits of a document for your purpose, confident that you can ignore the rest without risking missing something important. So where are the best places to look?

Signposting: Look at the document's signposting first – the features that can help you navigate your way through it. These could include its title, subtitle, standfirst, executive summary, conclusions or findings or recommendations, section headings, bullet points, lists, boxes, captions. Between them, they can help you or your enquirer to locate the parts where the information you need is most likely to be found.

Let's look at some of these features in more detail and try to decide how helpful they can be.

Titles and sub-titles may be helpful in determining the document's likely relevance overall. Main titles are frequently just there for effect – to provoke the reader into exploring the document further – but the sub-title can be a handy guide to its content or argument.

Blurbs (on the back cover or jacket flaps) can be a helpful guide to the contents too; but they are also a sales puff, and you even find them on many official or not-for-profit documents as well as commercial ones. So use only the facts and ignore the hype.

Contents pages can help you decide how you're going to navigate your way through the entire document. Look out in particular for sections that give the document's conclusions, recommendations or findings. (We'll come back to these in a minute.)

Abstracts are obviously a good place to try – particularly when you're dealing with a lengthy academic or professional article. But do bear in mind that there are two kinds of abstract: indicative abstracts, which merely tell you what the document is about; and informative abstracts, which should be a small but perfectly formed version of the original. At this stage in the process, only the latter are likely to be really useful to you. Also, many abstracts are written by the article's author; that person will no doubt be an expert in their field of study – but that doesn't necessarily mean that they can write a decent abstract that succinctly tells you everything you need to know and leaves nothing crucial out.

Executive summaries can be even more useful than abstracts because they're likely to go into more detail while still being short enough to be read in a few minutes. However, a complete executive summary is likely to be too long for you to just drop into your report whole, so you'll probably need to summarize the summary before using it – ensuring that you don't over-simplify in the process. And there's another potential downside to relying on an executive summary: they reflect the agenda of the author of the original document, which may or may not be the agenda of your enquirer. An executive summary could even quietly ignore inconvenient truths that lie buried within the document itself (just think of the 'Dodgy Dossier' that triggered Britain's participation in the Iraq war). So you'll need to be sure that the executive summary really does fairly represent the content as a whole.

Prefaces or Introductions are frequently not a lot of use. Authors often haven't a clue what to say in a preface or introduction. They may decide to use it to explain how the document came to be written, or to acknowledge the help and support they received – or sometimes it just contains platitudes from the head of the organization putting the report out. In fact, you might sometimes suspect that the author is using this section of the document to work out what they want to say. On the other hand, by the time they've reached the end of the document, they may possibly have worked out what that is, and be able to say it there fairly coherently.

Headings within articles or chapters can be helpful in determining which bits of a document you may need to read in more detail – particularly if you suspect that the abstract or executive summary may be missing something crucial, either accidentally or by design. Beware, however – sometimes headings are simply a typographical tool to help break up the text, and bear no relation to the structure of the document at all; editors can sometimes be so concerned about the appearance of the content on the page that they may require an author to insert a spurious heading at some point, even if there's no change of topic in the text.

Conclusions, Recommendations, Findings are likely to be the best place to discover what the document is saying, in a form succinct enough to be adapted pretty easily for your final report to your enquirer. Look out for alternative words or phrases that could mean the same thing – 'Results', 'Next Steps', 'Action Points', 'Lessons Learned' for example. So valuable can a section like this be that it's worth looking for it before considering any other part of the document. So – counter-intuitively, perhaps – the best place to start looking in any document is often at the end.

As we saw in Chapter 4 on Smarter Searching, there's sometimes no alternative to dipping into the full text – reviewing perhaps page after page of undifferentiated print with no headings or any other signposting features. So now might be a good time to go back to that chapter and check up on some of the straightforward scanning techniques that you can deploy – or recommend.

Finally – bearing all that in mind, we can at last move on to . . .

Capturing the content for your report

Back to your trusty matrix. First of all, there's one further refinement that you may have decided to make: sub-classify your priority scores so as to arrange your Must Know documents in the order in which you want to write them up. Having done that, you can then drop into the Summary & Notes column extracts taken from those documents – selected text that acts as a surrogate for the original and will form the basis of your (or your student's) narrative report. It's for you to decide in each case, of course, but you'll probably only need to do this for the Must Know documents. If you're actually doing the desk research yourself, think back to the elevator pitch; the likely purpose of your narrative report will be to introduce your enquirer to the key issues and findings, as a preliminary to presenting the results of your search in a logical and accessible way through the matrix. (And, as we'll see in a moment, brevity is a specific value that you can add to your report.)

At this stage, you'll also need to decide how you're going to handle the Should Know and Could Know documents. You may decide, for example, that you will simply indicate the scope of the Should Know documents and not go into them in any detail. So in this case you could restrict yourself to reporting that you found more specialized documents covering asylum seekers, housing, health and social care, and others documenting the particular experiences of Poles, Italians and Roma. With the Could Know documents, you might simply say briefly that your search also retrieved further items which for various reasons you regarded as being of lesser importance in answering the original enquiry.

However you decide to deal with these documents of lesser importance, they certainly won't be wasted, because you can still supply the entire matrix to your enquirer. That will give them, in an easily digestible form, an outline of all the documents – now considerably enhanced by the value you've added through classifying them according to their usefulness.

The same sorts of principles apply with the Should Know and Could Know documents if you're a student – albeit with perhaps a different approach. Faced with the need to demonstrate their knowledge to their assessor, the student may well want to provide a narrative that covers the Should Know documents as well as the Must Know. If so, then they'll need to apply exactly the same strategic reading techniques to the Should Know documents as well. When it comes to the Could Know documents, they may decide not to write these up in detail in their assignment report – but they can still cite them in the bibliography, or list them as 'other documents consulted'. (Oh, and while we're on the subject, you may have noticed that the citations of the two articles in the matrix above are not consistent. Assessors of student work can often be very hot on that, so it's certainly worth advising your student to check which citation style they're required to use and amend each of the citations accordingly – or use reference management software to do so.)

So – having decided all that – let's go back for the last time to our trusty matrix. By this stage, we've sub-classified the Must Know documents so they appear in the order in which we want to write them up. (I've just shown the first five of them here.) Now, using our strategic reading techniques, we've visited all the Must Know documents again to insert key text from each into the Summary & Notes column.

Priority	Topic	***	Title	Author	***	***	Summary & Notes
1.1	A: Population	***	2011 Census: Migration statistics for Wales	Office of National Statistics	***	***	Statistical estimates classifying people and households in areas of Wales and those having moved within Wales in the year before the Census
1.2	A: Population	***	Migration Statistics: Wales 2011	Statistics for Wales	***	***	Wales has experienced an estimated net inflow of migrants every year from mid-1998 to mid-2011, with an average net inflow of just over 9 thousand people per year. Annual net inflows have fluctuated though and decreased overall since 2006–07. Wales had a net inflow of international migrants between 1994 and 2010. In 2011 there was a net outflow of international migrants for the first time since 1993, with those leaving exceeding those moving to Wales by around 1.5 thousand persons.

Priority	Topic	***	Title	Author	***	***	Summary & Notes
							For years ending mid-1999 to mid-2011 there was a net inflow of migrants to Wales from the rest of the UK of around 6.5 thousand people per year on average. Over this period the net inflow decreased from 14.4 thousand persons in year ending mid-2003 to 2.5 thousand in years ending mid-2010 and mid-2011. On average the South West experienced a net inflow of migrants from the other regions of Wales while North Wales experienced a net outflow of migrants to the other regions of Wales between mid-2007 and mid-2011
1.3	C: Economic	***	Statistics on migrant workers in Wales	Statistics for Wales	***	***	According to the Annual Population Survey (APS), there were 74,000 employed Welsh residents in 2008 that were born outside the UK, or 5.5 per cent of all employed Welsh residents. This number increased by 22,000 or 42 per cent between 2004 and 2008. Most of the increase was accounted for by A8 nationals, but there were also increases amongst people born outside Europe. The latest data from the Annual Population Survey, covering calendar year 2008, shows 13,500 employed residents in Wales born in the A8 countries, up over 12,500 since 2004. Two-thirds of Welsh residents who were born in the A8 countries are aged between 16 and 34, compared to less than a quarter of residents who were born in the UK. Five local authorities account for nearly two-thirds of the applications to the Worker Registration Scheme in Wales (Carmarthenshire, Flintshire, Newport, Wrexham and Cardiff). These authorities have also seen the highest number of NINo applications from A8 nationals. Two-thirds of applications to the Worker Registration Scheme in Wales have been from Poland, with a further sixth from Slovakia
1.4	B: Social	***	Immigration and inclusion in South Wales	Joseph Rowntree Foundation	***	***	For new migrants, economic integration seemed a necessary precursor for inclusion and cohesion; those who were able to work were viewed more favourably by settled populations. There was no evidence that community tensions are an inevitable consequence of new immigration. Age-based and generational tensions of different kinds existed across all the groups and geographical areas studied. Poverty and deprivation had a direct and negative impact on inclusion and cohesion in the case study areas. Social class differences were a complex but important factor in shaping people's experiences of inclusion and cohesion and in shaping community responses to new migration.

Priority	Topic	***	Title	Author	***	***	Summary & Notes
1.5	C: Economic	***	Globalization and its impact on Wales	House of Commons Welsh Affairs Committee	***	***	As national economies become ever more integrated into the global market, new opportunities arise for people to move abroad, either to settle or to spend a section of their career working in another country. This is manifested not only in population movement into Wales, but also in the decisions of Welsh people to leave the country and work elsewhere. As globalization continues and even accelerates, these flows are likely to continue, although the rate and nature of movement will vary over time. Wales must therefore prepare for an economic climate in which its workforce is viewed as a global resource.

Now you're ready to write!

So you now have the best bits of each of your Must Know documents copied into the Summary & Notes cell at the right hand end of your matrix. You may still want to use this content selectively – just taking the first sentence of each of the paragraphs for example – but you may well be able to simply copy and paste your selected content into your report document, in the priority order in which you want to present it. But if you were able to do this, would that be plagiarism? Not if you do the copying responsibly (or your student does). Plagiarism is copying someone else's work without acknowledgement and passing it off as your own – whereas the responsible researcher or student would always acknowledge the source of their information.

You may originally have thought that creating the draft would be the most laborious part – but, as we'll see now, it can actually be one of the simplest and most straightforward stages, leaving you (or your student) with time to polish that draft and turn it into a really worthwhile literature review or student assignment report. However, it is worth giving some thought to how you're going to tell your story, because there are several tried and tested story-telling techniques you could consider. Try these . . .

Timeline

This is probably the most straightforward story-telling technique. There will be many occasions when you've simply arranged your retrieved documents by date, and a natural progression from the earliest development to the latest seems the obvious form for your story to take. However, it does mean that you're giving your enquirer the oldest information first – information that may well have been superseded by later developments. You could alternatively tell your story in reverse chronological order – giving the latest information first. Better perhaps, though, to start with the most important information (which will in all probability be the latest) and add further detail not according to its increasing age but to its relevance to the main result. (See the Inverted Pyramid below.)

Tell them . . . tell them . . . tell them . . .

In other words: tell the enquirer what you're going to tell them (remind them of the subject of the search); then tell them the actual story (summarize the Conclusions, Recommendations, Findings or whatever other part of each document you've decided to use as the surrogate); and finally tell them what you've told them (repeat the key result as confirmation). We've already come across this technique in Chapter 6, when we looked at ways of presenting an answer orally. This is a good technique for that purpose, giving the enquirer a little bit of time at the start to get onto your wavelength. (It's a technique beloved of trainers – and, by the way, it's also the story form used for each of the chapters of this book.) However it may be too cumbersome for a short written summary. So instead how about . . .

Inverted pyramid

With this structure, you give the most important finding first (i.e. the headline result) and then gradually add further supporting detail, working from the most important to the least, so the enquirer can decide when they have read enough. Again, we've seen this technique in action in Chapter 6, when providing oral answers. As we discovered, it's the classic way of telling a news story – put the climax first and then add the supporting details, starting with the most important ones. It's a good story-telling technique to use if your search has produced one overwhelmingly significant finding.

Thesis, antithesis, synthesis

The story structure here is 'On the one hand . . . On the other hand . . . On balance . . .' and it's often a very good one to employ when you're reporting on research findings. Such searches frequently produce contrary results but also indicate a degree of consensus between the extremes. In fact, whatever your topic, search results often come out in this form, so this can be an ideal way of summarizing them.

What might your draft look like?

So, based on the decisions you've taken so far, you might end up with a draft report that looks something like this . . .

The 2011 Census provides statistical estimates classifying people and households in areas of Wales and those having moved within Wales in the year before the Census. Wales has experienced an estimated net inflow of migrants every year from mid-1998 to mid-2011, with an average net inflow of just over nine thousand people per year. Annual net inflows have fluctuated though and decreased overall since 2006–07.

According to the Annual Population Survey (APS), there were 74,000 employed Welsh residents in 2008 who were born outside the UK, or 5.5 per cent of all employed Welsh residents. This number increased by 22,000 or 42 per cent between 2004 and 2008.

For new migrants, economic integration seemed a necessary precursor for inclusion and cohesion; those who were able to work were viewed more favourably by settled populations.

As national economies become ever more integrated into the global market, new opportunities arise for people to move abroad, either to settle or to spend a section of their career working in another country. Wales must therefore prepare for an economic climate in which its workforce is viewed as a global resource.

So what story form is this? It's not always possible to be precise, but it's probably closest to the Inverted Pyramid: providing the headline finding first; then adding detail about migrant workers and their social integration; and finally looking ahead to the implications of globalization for future migration.

Crucially, though, it's extremely easy to draft. If you check back to the final matrix, you'll find that it consists of the first sentence or two of each of the summary texts (and the last sentence of the final item as well). So at this stage it's simply a copy-and-paste job. You may even decide that you can hand it over to your enquirer (along with the matrix) with no further revision. More often than not, though, you'll decide that it's not quite good enough yet.

Editing – polishing your draft

Since it is probably a copy-and-paste job at this stage, your draft could well look disjointed – reflecting the different writing styles of the various authors of the originals and lacking crucial linking text between the selected document summaries. Nevertheless, you should have been making efficient use of your time up to now, and have built into your schedule plenty of time to polish your draft before submitting it. As always, these are techniques that you may be applying yourself or else they constitute good practice that you can pass on to your students. Whichever it is, there are some really good editing principles you can apply to ensure that your final draft reads as coherently and as fluently as possible. So either ask yourself or your student about . . .

Brevity

Can you shorten your report while still retaining all the detail? Alternatively, have you included more detail than is necessary at this stage? So check to see whether you've included any phrases (or names of institutions or concepts) more than once in full; if so, shorten or remove the second and subsequent instances. Also look for redundant words – particularly those that don't add anything to the sense of what you're saying. Adverbs are a good place to start.

Readability

Do the words you've used read like comprehensible spoken English? Will your report sound fluent when your enquirer vocalizes it inside their head? (We all tend to do this no matter how literate we consider ourselves to be – so you can, for example, make it a lot easier for your reader by providing complete sentences rather than notes.) And this is of course also the time when you decide whether the style of phrases or sentences that you may have copied direct from your matrix matches that of the rest of your report.

There are more ways in which you (or your student) can improve a report's readability too. You can replace any jargon or bureaucratic language with plain English (but do keep any precisely defined scientific or technological terminology). And you can change passive sentences or phrases into the active voice; this will either shorten and clarify the sentence or tell a more complete story – or possibly even both.

Another good thing to do is ask a critical friend to read your report; with a fresh pair of eyes, they'll almost certainly be able to suggest improvements, or even spot howlers that you've missed. Alternatively, if there's no one available to do this for you, try to put the report aside for a while – over a lunch break or even overnight – and then read it again yourself. And the final test of a document's readability is to read it aloud; does it sound like decent English now, or are bits of it gobbledegook? Reading it aloud will probably tell you.

Relevance

We've already looked at this issue in Chapter 6. As with every answer you provide – whether oral or written – you need to check that you've covered every aspect of the enquirer's search request. So check back to the original wording of the request (as agreed between you and the enquirer) to determine whether you need to try an additional supplementary search.

Retrievability

If you're working in a research environment, you may already be storing your search reports in a retrieval system such as a know-how file. If you are, or if you're planning to do so in the future, you'll need to be sure that your report is findable again when required. So consider adding a final section listing relevant keywords or phrases that you haven't been able to include in your summary text. If you do this, try to include terms that are synonymous, broader, narrower or otherwise related to the words and phrases you have used in your report. (Check back to Chapter 4 on Smarter Searching for a reminder of the issues involved.)

Making sure your work gets read and valued

Spare a thought for a moment for the poor decision-maker in whose in-tray your report is now languishing – or the weary lecturer faced with a pile of student assignments to mark. They may have spent all day looking at document after internal document all presented in 11pt Calibri with the margins set at 2.54 cm all round. Small wonder if they don't give your or your student's *magnum opus* the attention you think it deserves. Just a little bit of further enhancement can ensure that your work gets read and valued.

As we've already seen in Chapter 6, this isn't an optional extra but a vital aspect of the way you promote your service. We looked there briefly at how you could enhance the look and feel of your documents (or encourage your students to). But now's the time to think in more detail about things you could do. So think about . . .

Branding

Put your institution's logo in the header or footer section of your report. Do this once in a template or 'shell' document which you use as the basis for all your reports and you'll never have to think about it again. Add the name of your service prominently adjacent to the logo. And perhaps create a strapline to encapsulate your service's unique selling proposition (USP).

Disclaimer

You may need to include a note indicating the limitations of your report – perhaps emphasizing that it is based solely on the evidence of the documents retrieved and not on background knowledge of the subject concerned. You can find plenty of examples of disclaimer wordings online, and probably in collections of legal forms and precedents as well. If in any doubt, consult your organization's legal department.

Design and layout

Don't use your word processing package's standard default fonts. Instead use your institution's house style font if you can – or else pick a pair of pleasing complementary fonts (serif for headings, sans serif for text perhaps). Incorporate your organization's corporate colours into your design. (Ask your design department for the exact Pantone or RGB numbers to use so you can match the shades precisely.) Use colour highlighting for headings and subheadings – and instead of using the pre-set margins, try one of the following . . .

Columns allow you to squeeze a lot of text into a small space without it looking too crowded (but they're not really suitable for on-screen reading).

Dropped top margins with wide line spacing can give a short report a spacious, stylish, authoritative look (and a generous left-hand margin can provide space for the enquirer to make notes).

Concealed tables (with the border lines removed) are much better than tabs for creating more complex lay-outs, because they ensure that all the text and other graphic elements in your document stay where you want them.

Of course your organization may have a powerful corporate design department, staffed by fearsome style police who refuse to allow you to deviate even fractionally from the approved corporate look-and-feel. If this is the case, it's probably not worth trying to oppose or circumvent it. Instead, perhaps try befriending the design department, seeking advice from them on how you can improve the impact of your reports while still conforming to corporate style guidelines.

Symbols

Using symbols to denote, for example, different types of information or document status can give a lift to the visual appearance of your report. You could use some of the symbols supplied with your word processing package, or perhaps get royalty-free clip art from the web. Beware though! If you do decide to do this, make sure you use it sparingly and subtly. Unimaginative or facile use of clip art can actually detract from the enquirer's perception of your work's value.

Hyperlinks

Obviously you can add an enormous amount of value to your report by including live links to the original documents where possible, so that the enquirer can look at items of particular interest straight away. However, there is a slight risk that, having clicked on a particularly interesting link, the enquirer never comes back to your report at all. So rather than including the live links in the text of your report, you could include the references to the original documents as footnotes.

You can also make good use of internal links if your summary is quite lengthy. So consider including a contents list with links to the various sections of your report (and frequent links back to the top as well of course).

Enquirer feedback

As we've already established in Chapter 6, one crucial link that you should provide in every report is to a place where the enquirer can provide feedback. This could be a simple word-processed form somewhere on your intranet, or you could use web-based survey software. Either way, it's a crucial part of the **review** stage of the POWER model, where you reflect on the effectiveness of the work you've just done and consider how you might improve on it in the future. (For more on performance review, go back to Chapter 6.)

Protecting your design

Finally, send your report as a PDF rather than a word processed document. That will ensure that it reaches the enquirer looking as good as it did when it left you.

Coming next – choosing your toolkit

We've come a long way in this book so far – from complete mystery as you took the initial enquiry, with perhaps only the haziest idea as to how to solve it, to providing a polished, value-added narrative answer now (or helping others to do so). But one thing we've hardly done at all so far is consider any specific sources or other tools that might help you to achieve this.

That's been deliberate. The focus of this book is on the thinking skills that you can bring to bear when handling enquiries, irrespective of the subject matter of the enquiry or your knowledge of any sources that might provide an answer. But in the last chapter we're going to consider a whole range of tools that could help you: enquiry management systems to enable you to keep track of your query workload; library management systems to help you discover resources within your own collections; other search engines as possible alternatives to the market leader; reference management systems to help you manipulate and prioritize your search results. And above all, multipurpose information sources to help you get started on a wide range of enquiry types.

But we're still not losing sight of the fact that the best single tool you have at your disposal is your ability to think your way out of problems. So we'll also be considering how you can best deploy three crucial tools when creating or developing an enquiry service: time, intellect and money. The time you spend at work is (hopefully) constrained, and your budget certainly will be. But your intellect is limited only by your own imagination. So, besides check-listing tools that can help you answer enquiries better, we'll also learn about deploying predictive thinking skills to work out how you can best serve your enquirers.

To recap . . .

- **Remember POWER and KISS.**
- **Turn your raw search results into a dataset you can manipulate.**
- **Must Know, Should Know, Could Know can help you select, reject and prioritize.**
- **Use strategic reading to find the best material for your report, and decide on the best structure for your story.**
- **Good design gets your work noticed and acted upon.**
- **Your critical thinking skills enable you to achieve all this quickly and efficiently.**

CHAPTER 8

Choosing your toolkit

Using your predictive thinking skills to determine the resources you'll need

In this chapter you'll find tools to help you:

- **keep track of your enquiries**
- **discover information buried in your own resources and beyond**
- **choose the right search engine and use it well**
- **add value to your search results**
- **get started on each enquiry**
- **exercise your predictive thinking skills when deciding what to acquire.**

'Give us the tools and we will finish the job', said Winston Churchill famously during World War 2 – and that's the stage we've reached too. Up to now we've tended not to mention specific sources or products by name but just to refer to them generically. This is a manual about skills, after all – not a sourcebook. But if you've stuck with us this far, you'll be aware that we've referred to search engines, enquiry tracking systems, library management systems and the discovery facilities they can offer, reference management software – and above all specific information sources that can get you started on a whole range of enquiries. So this final chapter includes links to a selection of resources that you might find useful in your enquiry work. None of the lists in this chapter are exhaustive, and professional peers may dispute some of the choices. But hopefully they'll be enough to give you a flying start.

But before we launch into those, we still mustn't lose sight of the fact that the best single tool at your disposal is your ability to think your way from problem to solution. We've seen that at work throughout the book, and it applies just as much when you're planning a shopping expedition for resources that can help you in your enquiry work. It should be pretty obvious, really, that you can't reach any decisions on how to tool up until you've worked out what your enquirers are likely to need and the demands you can expect them to put on your service. This is true whether you're providing information to the public, to an academic community or to your colleagues and clients in a specialist organization. It requires some detailed thought before you take any irrevocable decisions, and brings in yet another thinking skill: predictive thinking.

Making best use of your Time, Intellect and Money

Every service you provide, and every tool you acquire, is likely to consume three principal resources in different degrees: your **Time**, your **Intellect** and (of course) your organization's **Money**. Clearly everything you do involves money in terms of the time you devote to each task. But only one of these three involves hard cash – the one resource that is overtly limited in terms of your budget – and that's Money. The other two resources are limited only by your ability. You can limit the Time you devote to different aspects of your work by working smarter, and by sweating your assets – the resources you have decided to invest Money in. And to achieve that, you need to deploy your tried and tested thinking skills – in other words, your Intellect. Call it the TIM test, if you will.

Let's suppose, for example, that you're setting up a new information service to meet the needs of a specialist organization – a research body, government agency, not-for-profit organization, charity, professional practice or commercial company – or that you're reviving a run-down service in one of these. How might the TIM test work in planning your service? Well, you may have initially identified five goals:

1 Find out what your users need.
2 Identify and acquire sources that will meet those needs.
3 Exploit your sources to ensure they earn their keep.
4 Promote your service by taking it out to your existing users and cultivating new ones.
5 Get help and support to allow you to develop in your job.

You'll then have thought about what you need to do to achieve each of these goals – and it's that activity that will consume your three resources of Time, Intellect and Money, in varying degrees. Like this, perhaps . . .

1 Find out what your users need

ACTIVITIES	Time	Intellect	Money
Meet the decision makers in your organization. Consider the special requirements of departments such as Research, Business Development, Competitive Intelligence, External Relations or Risk Management.	Quite a lot to start with. The various meetings could take some time to set up and will require careful preparation and probably follow-up afterwards as well. You may also need to manage expectations of what you can achieve.	You'll need to think carefully about the questions you're going to ask each head; these will vary depending on each department's role.	None

2 Identify and acquire sources that will meet those needs

ACTIVITIES	Time	Intellect	Money
Look for sources that will help you discover: 1 What's going on in your organization's specialism now 2 Who the major players are 3 How they are communicating with each other 4 How to find out about earlier developments.	Again, quite a lot: exploring source guides to help you identify possible publications, databases, websites and social media; sampling and evaluating those resources; deciding what to purchase, subscribe to or join; acquiring them.	To answer the questions posed in the Activities box, you'll need to think about sources like: 1 Trade and professional media 2 Trade, industry or professional directories and bodies 3 Conference proceedings, discussion lists, specialist blogs 4 Professional and academic journals, conference papers, reports. You'll also need to decide whether to acquire these resources in print or electronic form or both.	Once you've reached your decisions on what to acquire, this is probably where the bulk of your money will go. (But don't ignore the possibility that many top-level reports may be free.)

3 Exploit your sources to ensure they earn their keep

ACTIVITIES	Time	Intellect	Money
Scan the trade media and professional journals for new developments. Set up automatic alerts or feeds where possible. Sign up to specialist blogs and discussion lists. Be ready to acquire individual documents on an ad hoc basis.	Depends on how much of the process you can automate – but, where you can't, these tasks could still represent a good investment of your time.	Particularly exploit the trade and professional media. Many news stories highlight new reports that you can acquire; articles and opinion pieces alert you to the hot issues; reviews help you identify core literature; ads lead you to potential suppliers or partners.	Not necessarily much new money; you've already spent most of it in acquiring the resources in the first place. However, purchasing reports and one-off articles will be a further drain on your budget.

4 Promote your service by taking it out to your existing users and cultivating new ones

ACTIVITIES	Time	Intellect	Money
Encourage your initial contacts to become your advocates and champions. Concentrate on users' needs, not your resources. Alert your users to new developments through current awareness, selective dissemination of information (SDI) and automatic feeds.	Be ready to devote time to cultivating potential new users introduced by your champions. Work out how you can minimize the time you spend on routine alerting activity. Automate as much as possible – e.g. by setting up direct alerts to interested users.	The more time you can save by automating routine information tasks, the more you have to devote to growing your service and carrying out the more complex enquiries that can enhance your service's reputation and prestige.	You may want to invest in specialist software to disseminate your information – but thereafter you're probably just exploiting resources that you've already paid for.

5 Get help and support to allow you to develop in your job

ACTIVITIES	Time	Intellect	Money
Locate fellow information workers. Join professional online forums. Join a professional association. Keep your skills up to date through reading professional literature and going on training courses.	You may find it difficult to devote time to this because of the constant pressures involved in delivering your own service. But try to set some regular time aside if you can – it will probably pay dividends in improving the service you can offer.	You'll need to think about the kind of support you need and how you can improve your own skills. Then imagine and identify the kind of individual, organization or document that might meet those needs.	Some of these activities will incur a cost. Your employer might help, but you may need – or even prefer – to invest your own money in your continuing professional development.

Of course, you probably won't agree with all the assessments made here – or even the need for all the activities. That's fine! It's merely designed to show the principle; the actual decisions are yours. Managers of academic or public libraries will have different priorities – so they may employ user surveys rather than meeting individual decision makers to determine their communities' needs – and if they use specialist survey services for that purpose that may or may not incur a cost. Academic libraries will lay much more emphasis on professional and academic journals than the table above shows, and public libraries will probably be more interested in free and community-based resources. But the principle of applying the TIM test still operates, whatever information environment you work in.

Keeping track of your enquiries

We saw in Chapter 2 that you can operate a much more efficient enquiry service if you use some kind of software package to help you manage your work. Automating your enquiry or research management gives you an audit trail in case of problems, and will provide useful performance data as well. So here are some software packages and services that are suitable for keeping track of enquiries. And not necessarily just library, information or research enquiries – they can potentially work for any organization providing customer services, whether administrative, technical or transactional. Their features, functionality, availability by country and delivery media do vary – so check them out individually if you want to follow any of them up.

Product	Available from . . .	Details at . . .
247lib.com	Applied Network Solutions	www.247lib.com
Enquire	OCLC	www.oclc.org/en-UK/enquire.html
EOS.Web Reference Tracking	EOS	http://eos.sirsidynix.com/modules/reference-tracking
Illumin	Softlink	www.softlinkint.com/product/illumin
KnowAll Enquire	Bailey Solutions	www.knowallenquire.co.uk
LibAnswers	Springshare	www.springshare.com/libanswers
Mosio for Libraries	Mosio	www.textalibrarian.com
QuestionPoint	OCLC	www.oclc.org/questionpoint.en.html
RefTracker	Altarama	www.altarama.com
RT: Request Tracker	PTFS Europe	www.ptfs-europe.com

Discovering information in your own resources (and beyond)

As we explained briefly in Chapter 4, your library management system (LMS) – designed to keep track of your acquisitions, cataloguing, loans and serials management – will include at the very least a simple search interface for your own online public access catalogue (OPAC). But it's quite likely that it will incorporate more sophisticated discovery tools as well. These could offer advanced searching and reference management facilities, support a wide range of outputs and include social features. They will probably enable you not only to source potentially useful material from within your own collections (whether formally published or internal) but also from the wider information world outside as well. Such tools may come as part of the LMS package or may be integrated offerings from third parties. So it's worth exploring your own LMS (or integrated library system – ILS) to see what searching or discovery tools it offers and assess their comprehensiveness and scope. Here are some to consider . . .

Product	Available from ...	Details at ...
247lib.com	Applied Network Solutions	www.247lib.com
Axiell Archives Libraries Museums	Axiell Ltd	http://alm.axiell.com
BLUEcloud	SirsiDynix	www.sirsidynix.com/bluecloud
Encore Discovery Solution	Innovative	www.iii.com/products/sierra/encore
Ex Libris Primo	ProQuest	www.proquest.com/products-services/Ex-Libris-Primo.html
Heritage Online	Heritage Cirqa	www.isoxford.com/heritage/opac
Inmagic GeniePlus	Lucidea	http://lucidea.com/inmagic-genieplus
KnowAll Web OPAC	Bailey Solutions	www.baileysolutions.co.uk/web-opac
Knowvation	PTFS Europe	www.ptfs-europe.com/knowvation
Liberty	Softlink	www.softlinkint.com/product/liberty
Library Search	Capita	www.capita-software.co.uk/libraries/fldbriefing
OLIB	OCLC	www.oclc.org/en-UK/olib/learn-more.html
Soutron Discovery	Soutron Ltd	www.soutron.com/industry-sectors/research
Summon Service	ProQuest	www.proquest.com/products-services/The-Summon-Service.html
SydneyEnterprise	Lucidea	http://lucidea.com/sydneyenterprise
VuFind	Villanova University Falvey Memorial Library	http://vufind-org.github.io/vufind/about.html

Choosing and using the right search engine

As we made clear in Chapter 4, there is more than one search engine! In fact there are hundreds. Internet searching expert Phil Bradley includes brief descriptions of around 200 on his website – some general-purpose but many highly specialized and potentially invaluable for hunting down specific types of web content such as acronyms, opening TV themes, rhymes, flags and symbols or Creative Commons documents. Meanwhile web trainer Karen Blakeman of RBA Information Services brings together details of the various advanced searching facilities available on leading search engines. So here are just a few places where you can find out more about available search engines and how you can use them better.

Resource	Available from ...	Available at ...
Internet Search Engines	Phil Bradley	www.philb.com/webse.htm
Which Search Engine When?	Phil Bradley	www.philb.com/whichengine.htm
Social Media Discovery Tools	Phil Bradley	www.philb.com/discovery.html
Search Tools: Summary and Comparison of Commands	RBA Information Services	HTML version: www.rba.co.uk/search/compare.shtml PDF version: www.rba.co.uk/search/ compare.pdf
Bing Commands	RBA Information Services	http://msdn.microsoft.com/en-us/library/ff795620.aspx
DuckDuckGo Syntax	RBA Information Services	https://duck.co/help/results/syntax
Google Advanced Search Operators	RBA Information Services	https://docs.google.com/document/d/ 1ydVaJJeL1EYbWtlfj9TPfBTE5IBADkQfZ rQaBZxqXGs

Adding value to your search results

In Chapter 7 we looked at how you could add enormous value to your raw search results by categorizing and prioritizing them and presenting them to your enquirer as a narrative report. We did acknowledge that, in the early stages, it could sometimes be a pretty labour-intensive and tedious activity – although the pain was probably worth the gain in terms of the outcome achieved. Nevertheless, the more of the process you can automate the better. Some of the library management systems listed above include features that allow you to add some value to the items you retrieve through their discovery tools. But you may also want to look specifically at reference management software. Designed for recording citations and generating bibliographies, it may also enable you to add further fields to each record to cover the additional characteristics you need to help you create your value-added report. Here are some to consider – but before you commit, do be sure that your chosen package will allow you to organize the records in the ways you need . . .

Product	Available from . . .	Details at . . .
EndNote	Clarivate Analytics	http://endnote.com
Mendeley	Elsevier	www.mendeley.com
RefWorks	ProQuest	www.proquest.com/products-services/refworks.html
Zotero	Roy Rosenzweig Center for History and New Media	www.zotero.org

Starter Sources

And finally, we suggested in Chapter 3 that you could function perfectly effectively by keeping in mind just a few multipurpose reference sources that between them could get you started on an incredibly wide range of enquiries. So now's the time to see what they are. Almost all of them are professionally edited, and one or more of them will frequently be your first port of call once you've imagined what the final answer will look like. Most of them are charged-for, although quite a few are free. Many are available in more than one medium – print, online, mobile, portable. Some are print only. They'll usually provide quality-checked information that you can rely on, and they can frequently also direct you to reliable websites as well. (The exception to this is the 'Finding Images' category; most of the sources listed here are only lightly edited, if at all.) Some sources have more than one use – so they'll crop up more than once in the Starter Sources list. Where a service is charged, the link shown here will usually take you to a description of it; if the service is free, the link will usually allow you to use it straight away. (However, free services may link to charged ones.)

Between them they should help you to find **documents** . . .

- basic reference sources
- books
- items to consult, borrow or buy
- journals and newspapers
- articles
- images (still and moving)
- . . . and also reliable material on unanticipated subjects.

. . . as well as **information** . . .

- facts and figures
- events, dates and news items
- statistics
- . . . and also possible **contacts** for further information.

The notes about their geographic coverage require a little clarification. The sources that claim world coverage frequently offer only patchy information about developing nations. 'American' coverage may mean just the USA or could include other North American countries. 'Europe' could refer to the whole continent, or the European Economic Area, or just the European Union. And coverage of 'Britain' sometimes also takes in Ireland or can be restricted to the British mainland. With all those caveats, try some of these . . .

Identifying basic reference sources

Try . . .	Coverage	Cost?	Details at . . .
Know It All, Find It Fast	UK-plus	Charged	www.facetpublishing.co.uk [Then follow links or use the site's search engine. Publication is print only.]
Know It All, Find It Fast for Academic Libraries	UK-plus	Charged	www.facetpublishing.co.uk [Then follow links or use the site's search engine. Publication is print only.]
Know It All, Find It Fast for Youth Librarians and Teachers	UK-plus	Charged	www.facetpublishing.co.uk [Then follow links or use the site's search engine. Publication is print only.]
New Walford Guide to Reference Resources 1. Science, Technology, Medicine 2. Social Sciences	World	Charged	www.facetpublishing.co.uk [Then follow links or use the site's search engine. Publication is print only.]
UlrichsWeb Global Serials Directory [Lists trade, industry and professional directories.]	World	Charged	http://ulrichsweb.serialssolutions.com

Identifying and tracing books

Try . . .	Coverage	Cost?	Details at . . .
British National Bibliography	UK	Free	www.bl.uk/bibliographic/natbib.html
Explore the British Library	World	Free	http://explore.bl.uk
Google Books	World	Free	http://books.google.com
Nielsen BookData	World	Charged	www.nielsenbookdata.co.uk

Tracing items to consult, borrow or buy

Try ...	Coverage	Cost?	Details at ...
Amazon [Items to buy]	World	Free	www.amazon.com
Google Books [Items to consult]	World	Free	https://books.google.com
Google Scholar [Items to consult]	World	Free	http://scholar.google.com
JSTOR [Includes open access e-books]	World	Charged	www.jstor.org
Microsoft Academic [Items to consult]	World	Free	https://academic.microsoft.com
WorldCat [Items to consult or borrow]	World	Free	www.worldcat.org

Identifying journals and newspapers

Try ...	Coverage	Cost?	Details at ...
UlrichsWeb Global Serials Directory	World	Charged	http://ulrichsweb.serialssolutions.com
Willing's Press Guide [Change the date in the web address for subsequent years.]	World	Charged	www.cision.co.uk/resources/white-papers/willings-2017-press-guide

Tracing and acquiring articles

Try ...	Coverage	Cost?	Details at ...
Arts and Humanities Full Text	World	Charged	www.proquest.com/products-services/Arts_and_Humanities.html
British Library On Demand	World	Charged	http://ondemand.bl.uk/onDemand/home
Ebsco	Single publisher	Charged	www.ebsco.com
Elsevier	Single publisher	Charged	www.elsevier.com
Emerald Insight	Single publisher	Charged	www.emeraldinsight.com
HW Wilson Databases	World	Charged	www.ebscohost.com/academic/h-w-wilson-databases
Ingenta Connect	Single publisher	Charged	www.ingentaconnect.com
JSTOR [Also covers open access e-books]	World	Charged	www.jstor.org
ProQuest Social Sciences Premium Collection	World	Charged	www.proquest.com/products-services/ProQuest-Social-Sciences-Premium-Collection.html

Try ...	Coverage	Cost?	Details at ...
ProQuest Technology Collection	World	Charged	www.proquest.com/libraries/academic/databases/tech_collection.html
Sage Journals Online	Single publisher	Charged	http://online.sagepub.com
Wiley Blackwell	Single publisher	Charged	www.wiley.com/wiley-blackwell

Finding images (still and moving)

Note: Unlike the sources in all the other categories, some in this category are only lightly edited, if at all.

Try ...	Coverage	Cost?	Details at ...
Blinkx [Moving images]	World	Free	www.blinkx.com
Flickr [Still images – registration required]	World	Free	www.flickr.com
Getty Images [Professionally edited commercial source of still images]	World	Charged	www.gettyimages.co.uk
Vimeo [Moving images]	World	Free	https://vimeo.com
YouTube [Moving images]	World	Free	https://www.youtube.com

Plus of course the image searching tools of generic search engines.

Finding reliable material on unanticipated subjects

Try ...	Coverage	Cost?	Details at ...
CORE [Open access research papers]	World	Free	http://core.ac.uk
Directory of Open Access Journals [Many journals searchable at article level]	World	Free	www.doaj.org
Google Scholar	World	Free	http://scholar.google.com
LexisNexis [Emphasis on business and law]	World	Charged	www.lexisnexis.com
Microsoft Academic	World	Free	https://academic.microsoft.com
ProQuest Databases	World	Charged	www.proquest.com/products-services/databases

Finding facts and figures

Try ...	Coverage	Cost?	Details at ...
CIA World Fact Book	World	Free	www.cia.gov/library/publications/resources/the-world-factbook/index.html
Euromonitor Passport [Emphasis on market research]	World	Charged	http://go.euromonitor.com/Passport-Home
Europa World Plus	World	Charged	www.europaworld.com/pub
Statesman's Yearbook	World	Charged	www.statesmansyearbook.com
Whitaker's Almanack	UK-plus	Charged	http://whitakersalmanack.com

Tracing events, dates and news items

Try ...	Coverage	Cost?	Details at ...
Keesing's World News Archive	World	Charged	www.keesings.com
Google News	World	Free	http://news.google.com

Plus thousands of news media, press agency, broadcast organization and expert blogger websites.

Identifying and tracing statistics

Try ...	Coverage	Cost?	Details at ...
Euromonitor Passport [Emphasis on market research]	World	Charged	http://go.euromonitor.com/Passport-Home
Eurostat	Europe	Free	http://ec.europa.eu/eurostat
Offstats: Official Statistics on the Web	World	Free	www.offstats.auckland.ac.nz
UK National Statistics	UK	Free	www.ons.gov.uk
United Nations Statistics Division	World	Free	http://unstats.un.org/unsd

Finding contacts for further information

Try ...	Coverage	Cost?	Details at ...
Associations Unlimited [Then follow links or use the site's search engine. Publication is available in print and online.]	World	Charged	www.gale.com
Europa World of Learning	World	Charged	www.worldoflearning.com
World Guide to Libraries [Then follow links or use the site's search engine. Publication is print/e-book.]	World	Charged	www.degruyter.com
Yearbook of International Organizations [Then follow links or use the site's search engine.]	World	Charged	www.uia.be/yearbook

Final word of warning

Information on sources and delivery media can go out of date incredibly quickly. As far as possible, we confirmed that all the information in this chapter was up to date at the time the book was published, but there may well have been changes since. If you can't trace a source listed in this chapter and would like to see if more up-to-date information is available, or if you discover that a link no longer works, contact the publisher, Facet Publishing, and ask to be put in touch with the author, Tim Buckley Owen.

Your goal: successful enquiry answering – every time

So that's it! With a little care and common sense – plus a rigorous exercising of your thinking skills – you can make enquiry answering one of the most satisfying and fulfilling work activities there is. The explosion of available information, the technological developments that can help you retrieve and enhance it, and the enormously increased awareness of the value of information – all of these combine to make the prospects for library and information professionals more exciting than ever before. What you need to do now is to grasp those opportunities. So the only thing that remains is to wish you success with your enquiry answering – every time.

To recap . . .

- **Make the most of your three key resources: Time, Intellect and Money.**
- **Plenty of software packages can help you manage your enquiries better.**
- **Administrative systems can help you discover information buried in your own collections and beyond.**
- **There is more than one search engine – check out the benefits and limitations of others.**
- **Bibliographic software can help you work more efficiently when adding value to your search results.**
- **Just a limited number of sources can get you started on a wide range of enquiries.**
- **And finally – use your predictive thinking skills to decide on the actual resources you'll need.**

Index

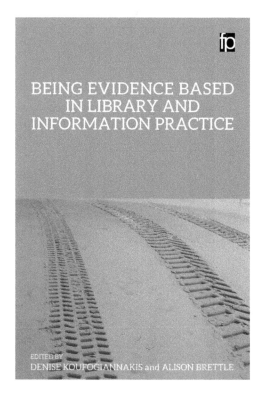